Ninja AF101 Air Fryer
Cookbook
for Beginners

**Effortless, Simple & Delicious Ninja Air Fryer
Recipes for Your Family & Friends**

Mavis Mitten

Contents

SNACKS & SIDE DISHES RECIPES 54

VEGETABLES & VEGETARIAN RECIPES 65

FAVORITE AIR FRYER RECIPES 79

INTRODUCTION

What Is An Air Fryer?

An air fryer is a gadget that is nothing but a mini convection oven - just like a regular oven but fits on your countertop. But as the name suggests, it uses air to fry and is no where close to a deep fryer.

You can cook almost anything like you would cook in an oven. The real benefit is that you use very little oil to produce crisp and great-tasting food.

Types Of Air Fryer

There are two different types of air fryers commonly used today and they are basket air fryers (square or cylindrical) or air fryer ovens also known as multi-functional air fryers or toaster air fryer ovens.

Both types work in similar ways, they are small, compact, and would only take up a small place on your counter. With an exception for Ninja air fryer which is somewhat bulky.

Regardless of the type you own, you will have these accessories

Basket (square or round) Your air fryer wouldn't work without one, it is important this comes complete in the box. This is attached to the air fryer basket base and can be detached with a click.
wire racks if you have an air fryer oven and a rositiere hook

How To Clean An Air Fryer?

This machine allows you to enjoy your favorite fried foods guilt-free and with less fat and fewer calories. But even when you're using it, you're still 'frying' after, therefore it's essential to clean it after every use since grease or oil build-up can make your device smoke.

Most models come with dishwasher-safe parts, so make sure to check the manual before washing. Here is how you clean an air fryer:

1. First refer to your manual on how to clean your specific gadget. Some brands have dishwasher safe parts.

2. Unplug your fryer from the electric socket.

3. Remove basket, pans, racks or any insert that has been used. Wash them with hot soapy water. If there is any food or baked-on grease, keep these parts to soak in the hot soapy water for 5 - 10 minutes before scrubbing them with a non abrasive sponge.

4. Now take a non abrasive sponge or a damp cloth with a little bit of dish soap to wipe down the insides of your air fryer. Wipe the soap away using a clean damp cloth.

5. The next step is to turn the appliance upside down and start wiping the heating element using a damp cloth. If there is any hard residue on the main part, apply a paste of water and baking soda on the baked-on, and scrub it slowly using a soft-bristle scrub brush.

6. Wipe the foam away using a clean and dry cloth.

7. Now it's time to clean the exterior of your air fryer. Simply, wipe it down using a damp cloth with some soapy water and then wipe the soap away with a clean & dry cloth.

8. Set the removable parts on the counter to dry before reassembling.

This is how simple it is to clean an air fryer. It is important to clean an air fryer after every use to keep it in good condition, and help it last more.

What You Should Know?

1. Don't forget to preheat the air fryer if need be. While this is not a deal-breaker, remember this gadget is a mini oven, some recipes might actually benefit from preheating the air fryer first. I mostly preheat when I am cooking frozen foods in the air fryer. It does help the food crisp up nicely.

2. Remember to shake or flip, this is important for even cooking.

3. Use an instant-read meat thermometer to make sure your food is cooked correctly to the right temperature.

4. Don't overload the basket with food, you will end up with a soggy mess and uneven cooking.

5. Make sure to clean the air fryer basket and base after each use. The accumulation of oil or crumbs is an accident waiting to happen and yes, it makes me judge you. CLEAN YOUR AIR FRYER AFTER EACH USE!!! To reduce the mess or clean up, you can line the base with foil.

6. Don't put parchment paper in the air fryer basket without weighing it down with food. If the parchment paper touches the heating element of the air fryer it can easily cause a fire hazard.

7. Don't detach the basket from the base whilst you are holding it up to avoid accidents. Only detach the basket when it is resting on a flat surface.

8. Remember to turn off the air fryer from the power supply when not in use

Pork, Beef & Lamb Recipes

Keto Steak Nuggets

Servings: 4 / Cooking Time: X Mins.

Ingredients:

- 1 lb. venison steak or beef steak, cut into chunks.
- 1 large Egg(s)
- Lard or palm oil for frying
- Keto Breading
- 1/2 C. grated parmesan cheese
- 1/2 C. pork panko
- 1/2 tsp. Homemade Seasoned Salt
- Chipotle Ranch Dip
- 1/4 C. mayonnaise
- 1/4 C. Sour Cream
- 1+ tsp. chipotle paste to taste
- 1/2 tsp. Homemade Ranch Dressing & Dip Mix
- 1/4 medium lime, juiced

Directions:

1. For the Chipotle Ranch Dip: Combine all ingredients, mix well. 1 tsp. of chipotle paste yields a medium-spice version, use more or less according to your own taste preferences. I encourage you to use my homemade ranch dressing and dip mix, it's superior to any store brought version. Refrigerate at least 30 minutes before serving, will keep for up to 1 week.

2. Combine Pork Panko, parmesan cheese and seasoned salt - again use my homemade not the store bought stuff. Set aside.

3. Beat 1 egg.. place beaten egg 1 bowl and breading mix in another.

4. Dip chunks of steak in egg, then breading. Place on a wax paper lined sheet pan or plate.

5. FREEZE breaded raw steak bites for 30 minutes before frying. This helps to ensure that the breading will NOT LIFT when fried.

6. Heat Lard to roughly 325 degrees F. Working in batches as necessary, fry steak nuggets (from frozen or chilled) until browned, about 2-3 minutes.

7. Transfer to a papertowel lined plate, season with a sprinkle of salt and serve with Chipotle Ranch.

Air-fryer Taco Twists

Ingredients:

- 1/3 lb. ground beef
- 1 large onion, chopped
- 2/3 C. shredded cheddar cheese
- 1/3 C. salsa
- 3 tbsp. canned chopped green chiles
- 1/4 tsp. garlic powder
- 1/4 tsp. hot pepper sauce
- 1/8 tsp. salt
- 1/8 tsp. ground cumin
- 1 tube (8 ounces) refrigerated crescent rolls
- Optional: Shredded lettuce, sliced ripe olives, chopped tomatoes and sliced seeded jalapeno pepper

Directions:

1. Preheat air fryer to 300°. In a large skillet, cook beef and onion over medium heat until meat is no longer pink; crumble meat; drain. Stir in cheese, salsa, chiles, garlic powder, hot pepper sauce, salt and cumin.

2. Unroll crescent roll dough and separate into 4 rectangles; press perforations to seal. Place 1/2 C. meat mixture in the center of each rectangle. Bring 4 corners to the center and twist; pinch to seal. In batches, place in a single layer on greased tray in air-fryer basket. Cook until golden brown, 18-22 minutes. If desired, serve with toppings of your choice.

Air Fryer Pork Chop Bites With Mushrooms

Servings: 4 / Cooking Time: 15 Mins.

Ingredients:

- 1 lb. (454 g) pork chops or pork belly , rinsed & patted dry
- 8 oz. (227 g) mushrooms (cleaned, washed and halved)
- 2 tbsp. (30 ml) Butter , melted (or olive oil)
- 1 tsp. (5 ml) Worcestershire sauce or soy sauce
- 1/2 tsp. (2.5 ml) garlic powder
- salt , to taste
- black pepper , to taste

Directions:

1. Preheat the Air Fryer at 400°F for 4 minutes. This will give a pork a nice sear.
2. Cut the pork chops into 3/4" sized cubes and combine with the mushrooms (or your favorite veggie). Coat the pork and mushrooms with the melted butter or oil, and then season with Worcestershire sauce, garlic powder, salt and pepper. Spread the pork and mushrooms in even layer in air fryer basket.
3. Air Fry at 400°F for 10-18 minutes, shaking and flipping and the pork belly 2 times through cooking process (time depends on your preferred doneness, thickness of the pork belly, size & cooking intensity of your air fryer).
4. Check the pork chop bites to see how well done it is cooked. If you want it more done, add an extra 2-5 minutes of cooking time.
5. Season with additional salt & pepper if desired. Serve warm, right away. If the pork bites get cold, they'll get tough.
6. NOTES
7. Air fryer sizes and styles vary, which will change cooking times. Keep checking the pork bites to make sure they are cooked the way you like them.
8. If cooking in multiple batches (if you have a small air fryer or are doubling the recipe), the first batch will take longer to cook if Air Fryer is not already pre-heated.
9. Remember to set a timer to shake/flip/toss the food as directed in recipe.

Go-to Pork Chops With Brown Sugar Rub In The Air Fryer

Servings: 4 / Cooking Time: 12 Mins.

Ingredients:

- 4 boneless pork chops about 1" thick
- Olive oil or avocado oil
- RUB
- 2 tbsp. brown sugar
- 1 tbsp. paprika
- 2 tsp. kosher salt
- 1½ tsp. ground black pepper
- 1 tsp. ground mustard
- ½ tsp. garlic powder
- ½ tsp. onion powder
- ¼ tsp. cayenne pepper optional

Directions:

1. Preheat the air fryer at 400°F/204°C for 5 minutes.

2. Mix the rub ingredients together.

3. Rinse and pat dry the pork chops.

4. Add a little olive oil to each of the pork chops to help the rub adhere to it.

5. Liberally massage the rub into both sides of the pork chops.

6. Place the 2 pork chops in the air fryer basket (if your basket is bigger and can hold more, go for it).

7. Cook for 10-12 minutes at 400°F/204°C, turning at the halfway point.

8. Make sure the internal temperature of the pork chop registers at 145°F/63°C before eating.

Cook Baby Back Ribs

Servings: X / Cooking Time: X Mins.

Ingredients:

- One tsp. of onion powder
- Two tsp. of chili
- A tray of baby back ribs
- 32-oz. grill sauce of any type
- One tsp. of grounded pepper
- One tsp. of brown sugar
- Half tsp. of garlic powder

Directions:

1. Preheat the fryer
2. Divide the ribs, by cutting, into relatively small pieces
3. Impeccably dry up the ribs using the towel
4. Take all the elements and mix them.
5. You should cook the ribs for about twenty minutes.
6. You may opt to brush some barbecue on the ribs once they adequately cooked.

Airfryer Kofta Kabab Recipe Low Carb

Servings: 4 / Cooking Time: 10 Mins.

Ingredients:

- 1 tbsp. Oil
- 1 lb. Lean Ground Beef
- ¼ C. Chopped Parsley
- 1 tbsp. Minced Garlic
- 2 tbsp. kofta kabab spice mix
- 1 tsp. Kosher Salt

Directions:

1. Using a stand mixer, blend together all ingredients. If you have time, let the mixture sit in the fridge for 30 minutes. You can also mix it up and set aside for a day or two until you're ready to make the kababs

2. Although I tried this with and without skewers, it really makes no difference to the final product. Since it's a lot easier to simply shape the kababs by hand, divide the meat into four and make four long sausage shapes (or Pokémon shape or whatever you want).

3. Place the kabals in your airfryer and cook at 370F for 10 minutes.

4. Check with a meat thermometer to ensure that the kabals have an internal temperature of 145F.

5. Sprinkle with additional parsley for garnishing and serve with tzatziki, a cucumber tomato salad, and pita bread.

6. TO MAKE IN AN OVEN

7. Preheat the oven to 375F as you begin preparations.

8. Line a small baking pan with foil and then place a rack inside the pan. Your kabals should be placed on the rack so that the fat drips down.

9. You may choose to finish them off with a broil.

10. To make on the grill

11. Preheat grill to 375F as you begin preparations.

12. Mix together ingredients in a stand mixer

13. Place meat on skewers

14. Grill until kabals reach an internal temperature of 145F

15. I used 85% ground beef but you can use any kind of meat you'd like including ground chicken, ground lamb, or a combination of beef and lamb which would be fabulous.

16. If you use lean ground meat such as venison, or bison, or turkey, you may need to add a little more oil and/or cook until just done and be very careful to not overcook.

Keto Pork Chops

Servings: 4 / Cooking Time: 20 Mins.

Ingredients:

- 4 1-2 Inch Thick Boneless Pork Chops
- 1 3 oz. Bag Pork Rinds, Crushed In The Food Processor
- 1 tsp. Kosher Salt
- 1 tsp. Smoked Paprika
- 1/2 tsp. Garlic Powder
- 1/2 tsp. Onion Powder
- 2 Large Eggs, Beaten

Directions:

1. In A Shallow Bowl, Mix The Crushed Pork Rinds With The Seasonings. In A Separate Shallow Bowl, Add In The Beaten Eggs. One At A Time, Coat The Pork Chops In The Egg, Then In The Pork Rind Mixture. Place The Breaded Pork Chops In The Air Fryer.

2. For 1 Inch Pork Chops, Set The Air Fryer At 400F For 12 Minutes And Flip Half Way Through. For 2 Inch Thick Pork Chops, Set The Air Fryer For 20 Minutes And Cook Half Way Through. Pork Chops Are Done When An Internal Temperature Thermometer Reads 145-160F.

3. Oven:

4. Place The Breaded Pork Chops On A Sheet Tray And Bake In A 425F Oven For 15 Minutes On Each Side Or Until An Internal Meat Thermometer Reads 145F.

Air Fryer Hamburger

Ingredients:

- 1 lb. 450g ground beef
- Salt
- Ground black pepper
- 4 slices of cheese
- 4 burger buns (gluten-free)
- Garnishes
- Tomatoes lettuce, mayo etc to your taste.

Directions:

1. Preheat the air fryer to 350F / 180C

2. Mix together the beef, salt and black pepper in a bowl.

3. Form the beef mixture in to four burger patties.

4. Spray the air fryer basket, add in the burgers.

5. Cook for 8-12 mins depending on your desired doneness and turn them half way through cooking.

6. When done, switch off the air fryer, top each patty with cheese, close the Air Fryer and let cheese melt on the burger for 1-2 minutes.

7. Build your burgers and then serve them

8. Don't forget to check the doneness of you hamburger by using this awesome Meat thermometer.

Air Fryer Steak Bites & Mushrooms

Servings: 4 / Cooking Time: 20 Mins.

Ingredients:

- 1 lb. (455 g) steaks , cut into 1" cubes & patted dry
- 8 oz. (227 g) mushrooms (cleaned, washed and halved)
- 2 tbsp. (30 ml) Butter , melted (or oil)
- 1 tsp. (5 ml) Worcestershire sauce
- 1/2 tsp. (2.5 ml) garlic powder
- salt , to taste
- Black pepper , to taste
- Minced parsley , garnish
- Melted butter for finishing , optional
- Chili Flakes , for finishing, optional

Directions:

1. Combine the steak cubes and mushrooms. Coat with the melted butter and then season with Worcestershire sauce, garlic powder, salt and pepper.

2. Preheat the Air Fryer at 400°F for 4 minutes.

3. Spread the steak and mushrooms in even layer in air fryer basket. Air fry at 400°F for 10-18 minutes, shaking and flipping and the steak and mushrooms about 3 times through cooking process (time depends on your preferred doneness, thickness of the steak, size of the air fryer).

4. Check the steak to see how well done it is cooked. If you want the steak more done, add an extra 2-5 minutes of cooking time.

5. Garnish with parsley and drizzle with optional melted butter and/or optional chili flakes. Season with additional salt & pepper if desired. Serve warm.

Bacon Avocado Fries

Servings: 24 / Cooking Time: X Mins.

Ingredients:

- ♦ 3 avocados
- ♦ 24 thin strips of bacon
- ♦ 1/4 c. Ranch dressing, for serving

Directions:

1. Save to my recipes

2. For oven

3. Preheat oven to 425°. Slice each avocado into 8 equally-sized wedges. Wrap each wedge in bacon, cutting bacon if needed. Place on a baking sheet, seam side down.

4. Bake until bacon is cooked through and crispy, 12 to 15 minutes.

5. Serve with ranch dressing.

6. For air fryer

7. Slice each avocado into 8 equally-sized wedges. Wrap each wedge with a strip of bacon, cutting bacon if needed.

8. Working in batches, arrange in air fryer basket in a single layer. Cook at 400° for 8 minutes until bacon is cooked through and crispy.

9. Serve warm with ranch.

Boneless Ribs Air Fryer Recipe

Servings: X / Cooking Time: X Mins.

Ingredients:

- Two stakes of unfrozen boneless ribs
- A little salt and black pepper for seasoning
- Olive oil

Directions:

1. Heat the air fryer to about 350 degrees.

2. Sauce the ribs.

3. Add some little salt and the black pepper to give it some taste.

4. Put the whole mixture in the air fryer and cook for about 10 minutes.

5. At the 10th minute, open and flip over the ribs to ensure proper cooking.

6. Use a thermometer to check if they cooked adequately.

Air Fryer Bacon Recipe

Servings: X / Cooking Time: X Mins.

Ingredients:

- Four strips of bacon that are cut into equal halves
- A little salt
- Preferably some black pepper (optional)

Directions:

1. Switch on your air fryer. Preheat it to about 375° for close to two minutes.

2. Pick each of the bacon halves and gently put them on the rack that comes with the fryer. This should ensure the slices of bacon are not sitting on the bottom.

3. Once done with the arrangements, cook the bacon for 8 to 12 minutes. Use tongs to ensure the portions of bacon stay in a single layer.

4. To ensure you attain a crispy taste, you can cook for a relatively more extended period.

5. Use the tongs to pick the bacon from the fryer. Ensure you put the bacon on some paper towel to allow it to drip the excess oil.

6. Serve with your favorite dish.

Simple Cowboy Casserole Dinner In The Air Fryer

Servings: 4 / Cooking Time: 15 Mins.

Ingredients:

- 1 lb. ground beef or ground turkey
- 1/4 C. yellow onion diced
- 1/2 tsp. salt
- 1/4 tsp. black pepper
- 1/2 C. frozen corn kernels
- 3/4 C. salsa
- 1/2 15 oz. can black beans pinto or white beans, drained and rinsed
- 1/2 C. cheddar cheese shredded
- 1 box Jiffy Cornbread or 1/2 of this homemade cornbread recipe.

Directions:

1. On the stovetop, brown the ground beef with the onion, salt and pepper, until fully cooked. Remove the grease from the ground beef. (Or, see air fryer instructions for cooking ground beef).

2. Combine the corn, salsa, and beans with the fully cooked ground beef.

3. Make the cornbread mixture according to its package directions.

4. Using an oven safe dish that will fit in your air fryer basket, (I used a 9x7 dish in my 5.8 Cosori air fryer), layer the ground beef mixture, then the cheese, then the cornbread batter. Be sure to evenly spread the the cornbread to the sides of the pan.

5. Place the pan in the air fryer. Cook for 15-17 minutes at 330 °F. If the cornbread starts to burn, cover it with foil so that it can finish cooking.

6. NOTES

7. Can I freeze cowboy casserole?

8. Double the recipe and freeze half of the meat mixture in a freezer safe bag to enjoy later.

9. When ready to use from the freezer, let the mixture thaw. Add it to the casserole dish, add the cheese, then cornbread mixture. Cook at the recommend temperature and time. You may need to add a couple of extra minutes if your meat mixture is still cold.

Air Fryer Zucchini Boats

Servings: 4 / Cooking Time: 10 Mins.

Ingredients:

♦ 1 lb. ground beef or ground turkey
♦ 1/2 onion diced
♦ 1/2 tsp. Italian seasoning
♦ salt and pepper to taste
♦ 12 oz. marinara sauce
♦ 2 medium zucchini
♦ parmesan cheese or other favorite cheese

Directions:

1. Make the marinara meat sauce that will go inside the zucchini boats by browning the ground beef. Add the onion, Italian seasoning, salt, pepper, and marinara sauce.

2. Take the zucchini, cut in half lengthwise and scoop out the seeds. Pat the inside dry with a paper towel. Lightly mist with oil and sprinkle with salt.

3. Place the zucchini in the air fryer basket and cook at 380°F/190°C for 8-10 minutes until cooked through. The cooking time will depend greatly on the size of your zucchini and how cooked through you want it to be. Check on the zucchini after 5 minutes and adjust as needed. Once your zucchini reaches its desired tenderness, pat dry any excess moisture from the zucchini, add the marinara meat sauce, sprinkle on parmesan cheese, and cook for an additional 2-3 minutes, or until cheese is melted.

4. Carefully remove from the air fryer basket and enjoy!

Bacon-roasted Potatoes

Ingredients:

- 1 1/2 lb. Small new potatoes (about 32), halved
- 4 sprigs thyme, plus 1 tsp thyme leaves
- 1 tbsp. Olive oil
- Kosher salt and pepper
- 3 slices bacon
- 3 medium shallots, cut into 1/4-in. Wedges
- 1 tbsp. White or regular balsamic vinegar
- 2 tsp. Whole-grain mustard

Directions:

1. In large bowl, toss potatoes and thyme sprigs with oil, ½ tsp salt and ¼ tsp pepper. Add to air fryer and top with bacon. Air-fry at 400°F until bacon is crisp, 6 to 12 minutes. Transfer bacon to paper towel and let cool before breaking into pieces.

2. Shake potatoes and continue to air-fry 8 minutes. Add shallots to basket with potatoes, toss to combine and air-fry until vegetables are golden brown and tender, 8 to 12 minutes. More.

3. Meanwhile, in large bowl, whisk together vinegar, mustard and thyme leaves. Transfer cooked vegetables to bowl, adding any oils from bottom of basket, and toss to combine; fold in bacon.

Fish & Seafood Recipes

Keto Coconut Shrimp

Ingredients:

- For the shrimp:
- 1 lb. shrimp peeled & cleaned
- ¾ C. all-purpose flour
- 1 tsp. each onion & garlic powder
- 2 eggs lightly beaten
- ½ C. each panko breadcrumbs & unsweetened shredded coconut flakes
- Kosher salt & fresh pepper
- Avocado or grapeseed oil
- ½ C. full fat mayonnaise
- Zest & juice of half a lime

- 1 clove garlic finely grated
- 2-3 tbsp. sriracha or hot sauce
- For the keto coconut shrimp:
- ¾ C. coconut flour
- 1 tsp. each onion & garlic powder
- 2 eggs lightly beaten
- ½ C. each pork rind crumbs & unsweetened shredded coconut flakes
- Kosher salt & fresh pepper
- Avocado or grapeseed oil

Directions:

1. For the keto coconut shrimp, prepare the dredge station by adding the coconut flour, onion & garlic powder, ½ tsp. salt, and a few cracks of pepper to a shallow dish, mix well. Add the eggs to a small dish/bowl and lightly whisk. Add the pork rinds to a zip-top bag and use a rolling pin to bash them into breadcrumbs the size of panko. Add them to a dish along with the coconut flakes, ¼ tsp. salt, few cracks of pepper, and mix well.

2. Season the shrimp with a little pinch of salt on bot sides then dredge in the coconut flour shake off any excess, dredge in the eggs, shake off any excess, dredge in the pork rind and coconut flakes and make sure the shrimp is well covered. Move shrimp to a wire rack set over a sheet tray. Repeat the process with the remaining shrimp.

3. For the regular version of the coconut shrimp, follow the same exact steps but you all-purpose flour instead of coconut, and panko breadcrumbs instead of pork rinds.

4. Pour 2 inches of oil into a frying pan and bring the temperature to 340-350 F. While the oil is coming to temperature, it's ok that the shrimp sit at room temperature so the coating ca firm up. Fry the shrimp in batches, for 2-3 minutes on each side, or until golden brown. Remove shrimp and place on a clean wire rack and fry the next batch.

5. Make the sriracha dipping sauce by combining all the ingredients in a small bowl and whisking well. Check for seasoning, you may need more sriracha if you like it spicy.

6. If using an air fryer to make the coconut shrimp, spray the basket with non-stick and fry for 8 minutes at 390 F, flipping the shrimp half way.

Healthy Fish Finger Sandwich & Optimum Healthyfry Air Fryer

Ingredients:

♦ 4 small cod fillets (skin removed)
♦ salt and pepper
♦ 2 tbsp flour
♦ 40g dried breadcrumbs
♦ spray oil
♦ 250g frozen peas
♦ 1 tbsp creme fraiche or greek yogurt
♦ 10–12 capers
♦ squeeze of lemon juice
♦ 4 bread rolls or 8 small slices of bread

Directions:

1. Pre-heat the Optimum HealthyFry Air Fryer.

2. Take each of the cod fillets, season with salt and pepper and lightly dust in the flour. Then roll quickly in the breadcrumbs. The idea is to get a light coating of breadcrumbs on the fish rather than a thick layer. Repeat with each cod fillet.

3. Add a few sprays of oil spray to the bottom of the fryer basket. Place the cod fillets on top and cook on the fish setting (200c) for 15 mins.

4. Whilst the fish is cooking, cook the peas in boiling water for a couple of minutes on the hob or in the microwave. Drain and then add to a blender with the creme fraiche, capers and lemon juice to taste. Blitz until combined.

5. Once the fish has cooked, remove it from the HealthyFry Air Fryer and start layering your sandwich with the bread, fish and pea puree. You can also add lettuce, tartar sauce and any other of your favourite toppings!

Coconut Shrimp With Spicy Marmalade Sauce

Servings: 4 / Cooking Time: 20 Mins.

Ingredients:

- 1 lb. large shrimp shelled and deveined
- 1/2 C. all purpose flour
- 1/2 tsp. cayenner pepper
- 1/4 tsp. kosher salt
- 1/4 tsp. fresh ground pepper
- 1/2 C. panko bread
- 8 oz. coconut milk
- 1 egg
- 1/2 C. shredded sweetened coconut
- for the sauce:
- 1/2 C. orange marmalade
- 1 tbsp. honey
- 1 tsp. mustard
- 1/4 tsp. hot sauce

Directions:

1. Rinse the shrimp and set aside.

2. Whisk together the flour, salt, pepper, cayenne and panko bread crumbs. Set aside.

3. In a small bowl, whisk the coconut milk and egg. Set aside. Fill a third shallow bowl with the shredded coconut.

4. One at a time, dip the shrimp in the flour mixture, the coconut milk and then, coat in the coconut.

5. Place shrimp in the basket of an air fryer and heat to 400°. Bake until shrimp is golden and cooked through, 10 to 12 minutes. Work in batches as necessary.

6. While the shrimp are cooking, whisk together the marmalade, honey, mustard and hot sauce.

7. Serve the shrimp with the sauce immediately.

Spicy Shrimp Lettuce Wraps

Servings: 6 / Cooking Time: 25 Mins.

Ingredients:

- 2 tbsp. Fresh lemon juice
- 1 1/2 to 2 Tbsp gochujang (Korean hot pepper paste)
- 1 tbsp. Olive oil
- 2 tsp. Honey
- 1 clove garlic, grated
- 2 tsp. Grated fresh ginger
- 1 1/2 lb. Large shrimp, peeled and deveined
- 1 head Boston lettuce, leaves separated
- 2 Persian cucumbers, sliced
- 1 bunch small radishes, sliced
- Mint and basil, for serving

Directions:

1. Heat oven to 425°F. In a large bowl, whisk together lemon juice, gochujang, oil and honey, then stir in garlic and ginger. Add shrimp and toss to coat.

2. Arrange in a single layer on a rimmed baking sheet and roast until just opaque throughout, 10 to 15 minutes.

3. Serve shrimp in lettuce and top with cucumbers, radishes, mint and basil.

Brown Stew Fish

Servings: 1 / Cooking Time: 10 Mins.

Ingredients:

- Rapeseed oil, for frying
- 1 whole snapper
- 1/2 onion, cut in rings
- 1 Scotch bonnet or habanero chilli pepper, whole
- 1 sprig thyme
- 125ml water
- 60ml olive oil
- 45ml fish and meat sauce
- 1 tomato, diced
- Salt and freshly ground black pepper

Directions:

1. Heat a deep-fryer with rapeseed oil to 180C. Deep-fry the whole snapper until lightly brown, approximately 4 minutes.

2. Saute the onion, pepper, thyme, water and olive oil in a large saute pan, for about 2 minutes. Add the fish and meat sauce and the fried fish.

3. Simmer for 5 minutes, then add the tomato and simmer for another 1 minute. Season with salt and pepper, to taste, and place on a serving platter.

Air Fryer Frozen Shrimp

Servings: 3 / Cooking Time: 10 Mins.

Ingredients:

- 1 lb. (454 g) frozen raw shrimp
- oil spray or vegetable oil , to coat shrimp
- salt , to taste
- black pepper , to taste

Directions:

1. Evenly coat the frozen shrimp with oil spray or vegetable oil. Season with salt & pepper (you do not need to thaw the shrimp).

2. Place the frozen shrimp in the air fryer basket and spread in an even layer (make sure they aren't overlapping).

3. Air Fry at 400°F/205°C for 8-14 minutes (depending on the size of your shrimp and your air fryer), flipping the shrimp halfway through cooking. Check for doneness & air fry longer if needed.

4. NOTES

5. Air Frying Tips and Notes:

6. Cook Frozen – Do not thaw first.

7. Shake or turn if needed. Don't overcrowd the air fryer basket.

8. If cooking in multiple batches, the first batch will take longer to cook if Air Fryer is not already pre-heated. Recipe timing is based on a non-preheated air fryer.

9. Recipes were tested in 3.4 to 6 qt air fryers. If using a larger air fryer, the recipe might cook quicker so adjust cooking time.

10. Remember to set a timer to shake/flip/toss as directed in recipe.

Air Fryer Frozen Fish Sticks

Servings: 2 / Cooking Time: 12 Mins.

Ingredients:

♦ 8 Frozen Breaded Fish Sticks

Directions:

1. Place the frozen breaded fish sticks in the air fryer basket. Make sure they aren't overlapping. No oil spray is needed.

2. Air Fry at 400°F/205°C for 8 minutes. Flip the fish sticks over and then continue to cook at 400°F/205°C for another 2-4 minutes or until cooked through and the coating is crispy.

3. NOTES

4. Air Frying Tips and Notes:

5. No Oil Necessary. Cook Frozen – Do not thaw first.

6. Don't overcrowd the air fryer basket. Lay in a single layer.

7. Recipe timing is based on a non-preheated air fryer. If cooking in multiple batches back to back, the following batches may cook a little quicker.

8. Recipes were tested in 3.7 to 6 qt. air fryers. If using a larger air fryer, they might cook quicker so adjust cooking time.

9. Remember to set a timer to flip/toss as directed in recipe.

Air Fryer Shrimp Scampi

Servings: 4 / Cooking Time: 10 Mins.

Ingredients:

- VEGETABLES
- 1/2 lb. asparagus
- 1/2 pint cherry tomatoes or 2 roma tomatoes o about 1/2 lb. of large tomato chunks
- 1/2 tbsp. olive oil
- 1/2 garlic clove minced
- salt and pepper to taste
- SHRIMP
- 1/2 lb. medium raw shrimp shelled, deveined, and tails off
- 1/2 tbsp. olive oil
- 1/2 tbsp. lemon juice

- 2 garlic cloves minced
- 1/8-1/4 tsp. paprika
- 1/8-1/4 tsp. onion powder
- 1/8-1/4 tsp. dried basil
- red pepper flakes to taste
- pepper to taste
- 2 tbsp. butter
- SERVE WITH (OPTIONAL)
- 1/2 lb. linguine
- lemon juice to taste
- parmesan cheese fresh and grated

Directions:

1. Make linguine according to package directions.
2. PREPARE THE Ingredients:
3. Wash and trim asparagus. Cut in half or thirds, depending on preference.
4. Wash tomatoes. If using Roma tomatoes, cut into bite size pieces.
5. If shrimp is frozen, thaw.
6. VEGETABLES
7. Combine the asparagus and tomatoes in a bowl with olive oil, garlic, salt and pepper. Stir until everything is evenly coated.
8. SHRIMP
9. Combine shrimp in a bowl with the oil, lemon juice, garlic, paprika, onion, basil, red pepper flakes, and pepper.
10. AIR FRY
11. Place the shrimp on one side of the air fryer basket. Place tomatoes and asparagus in the other side of the basket.
12. Air fry for 8 minutes at 380 °F.
13. Add about 2 tbsp. total of cubed butter to the top of the shrimp, asparagus, and tomatoes. Air fry for an additional 2 minutes.
14. SERVE AND ENJOY
15. Remove contents from the air fryer basket and combine with the cooked linguine in a bowl or plate. Take all the juices from the bottom of the air fryer basket and add to the pasta and shrimp. If you need additional liquid, add a little water.
16. Top with additional lemon juice and parmesan cheese, to taste and if desired.

Air Fryer Shrimp Cocktail

Servings: 6 / Cooking Time: 10 Mins.

Ingredients:

- FOR THE SHRIMP
- 1 lb. (455 g) raw shrimp , deveined and shells removed
- 1 tsp. (5 ml) oil , to coat shrimp
- salt , to taste
- black pepper , to taste
- SHRIMP COCKTAIL SAUCE
- 1/2 C. (120 g) ketchup (or low-carb tomato sauce for keto)
- 2 tsp. (10 ml) Worcestershire sauce
- 1 tsp. (5 ml) prepared horseradish
- 1 tsp. (5 ml) fresh lemon juice
- 1/4 tsp. (1.25 ml) celery salt
- 1/4 tsp. (1.25 ml) garlic powder
- 1/4 tsp. (1.25 ml) salt , or to taste
- black pepper to taste
- fresh lemon slices
- 1 (1) small cucumber , sliced (optional)
- fresh herbs for garnish (optional)

Directions:

1. In bowl, combine ketchup, Worcestershire sauce, horseradish, fresh lemon juice, celery salt, garlic powder, salt and black pepper. Stir until well mixed then set aside.

2. After shrimp shells are removed and de-veined, rinse and pat dry the shrimp. Coat shrimp with oil, and then season with salt and pepper. Place the shrimp in the air fryer basket or tray in a single layer.

3. Air Fry shrimp at 400°F for 8-12 minutes, or until cooked through. Shrimp comes in different sizes so check halfway through to make sure it's cooked enough or to your liking. After air frying, let the shrimp cool completely and chill in the fridge until ready to serve.

4. Serve the cooked shrimp with the shrimp cocktail sauce and slices of fresh lemon and cucumbers. Garnish with fresh herbs if you are feeling fancy.

Air Fryer Fish Recipe

Servings: X / Cooking Time: X Mins.

Ingredients:

- You can't afford to miss bread crumbs.
- For seasoning purposes, you will need lemon pepper.
- Have some little amount of salt to add taste to the crispy chicken.
- Garlic powder
- An egg? Yes, not one but two or more
- Finally, you can't miss fish fillets

Directions:

1. Start the whole process by mixing the bread crumbs with the seasoning
2. Bring in the egg and whisk it into the mixture.
3. Use the whisked egg in coating both sides of the fillet.
4. Put the coated fillet into the air fryer basket.
5. Leave to cook for some time before you spray with some olive oil.
6. Cook for about 10 minutes at about 350°.
7. Serve while still hot.
8. Conclusion
9. Cooking time is not fixed for every session. Depending on the thickness of the fish fillets, you may continue cooking for longer until you are satisfied the food is prepared adequately cooked.

Crunchy Fried Prawns With Spicy Mayo

Servings: 4 / Cooking Time: 10 Mins.

Ingredients:

- For the prawns
- 1 1/2 lb. prawns, peeled and deveined
- 1 C. buttermilk
- 1 egg, lightly beaten
- 1 tbsp. English mustard
- 1 tbsp. hot sauce
- 1/2 C. self-raising flour
- 1/2 C. yellow cornmeal
- 2 tsp. paprika
- Salt
- 1 tsp. cayenne
- 1 tsp. garlic powder
- Oil, for frying
- For the spicy mayo:
- 1 shallot, finely chopped
- 2 tbsp. finely chopped fresh parsley
- 1/2 tsp. cayenne pepper
- 3/4 C. prepared mayonnaise
- 2 tbsp. English mustard
- 1 tbsp. hot sauce
- Juice of 1/2 lemon

Directions:

1. Preheat deep fryer with peanut oil to 190°C.

2. Whisk together buttermilk, egg, and mustard in a casserole dish. In another casserole dish, whisk together flour, cornmeal, paprika, 2 tsp. salt, cayenne, and garlic powder.

3. Dredge prawns in the dry mixture then into the wet then back into the dry. Add prawns in batches to the deep fryer and fry until golden, about 2 minutes per batch. Serve with spicy mayo sauce.

4. Spicy Mayo:

5. Add the shallot, parsley, cayenne pepper, mayonnaise, mustard, hot sauce, and lemon juice to a bowl. Stir to combine. Chill until ready to serve.

Air Fryer Hot Crab Dip

Ingredients:

- 6.5 oz. (184 g) lump crab meat *see headnote, drained if necessary
- 8 oz. (227 g) cream cheese (1 package), softened
- 1 tbsp. (15 ml) fresh lemon juice
- 1/2 medium onion , diced
- 4 green onions , chopped
- 1 tbsp. (15 ml) Worcestershire sauce
- 1 C. (240 ml) mayonnaise
- 1/2 C. (50 g) freshly grated parmesan cheese
- 1 tsp. (5 ml) black pepper
- 1 tsp. (5 ml) minced parsley , for garnish
- FOR SERVING
- 4 wedges fresh lemon , for squeezing
- Chips, crackers, bread or for gluten-free serve with vegetables

Directions:

1. Spray the baking dish *see note below* with cooking spray or olive oil.

2. In large bowl, combine cream cheese, lemon juice, onions, green onions, Worcestershire sauce, mayo, parmesan cheese and black pepper. Gently fold in lump crab meat until it's combined into the cheese mixture.

3. Add the dip mixture into the baking dish. Place at the baking dish into the air fryer basket/tray.

4. Air Fry at 300°F/150°C for 20 minutes. After cooking for 20 minutes, stir the dip.

5. Continue Air Frying at 300°F/150°C for 10 minutes. Stir the dip again.

6. Increase heat to 340°F/170°C and then continue air frying for 5-10 minutes or until golden brown.

7. Top with minced parsley. Allow to cool for at least 10 minutes before serving. Serve with your favorite chips, crackers, bread or vegetables. Add a side of lemon wedges if you want if anyone wants to squeeze fresh juice on their serving.

8. NOTES

9. BAKING VESSELS

10. Find an oven-safe dip vessel to fit your air fryer basket or rack. One full batch will fit in a deeper 6.5"x3" baking dish. If your air fryer is too small or you only have smaller shallow baking dishes, cook the dip in two batches. If cooking anything less than the full volume of dip, cook for less time and keep checking until it's finished with a brown crust.

11. Baking ramekins also make great vessels to cook the dip in.

Air Fryer Parmesan Crusted Salmon

Servings: 4 / Cooking Time: 8 Mins.

Ingredients:

- 2 salmon fillets
- 1/4 C. mayonnaise
- 1 tsp herb and garlic seasoning
- shredded parmesan cheese to taste

Directions:

1. Preheat the air fryer at 400°F/204°C for 5 minutes.

2. Mix together the mayonnaise with the herb and garlic seasoning in a small bowl.

3. Pat dry the salmon fillets with a paper towel and place the salmon in a lightly sprayed air fryer basket or on top of a foil sling in an air fryer basket.

4. Spread the herb mayonnaise mixture on the top of the salmon filets. Top with parmesan cheese.

5. Cook in the air fryer at 350°F/175°C for 8 minutes, or until the salmon registers at 145°F/62.7°C with an instant read thermometer.

Air-fryer Pretzel-crusted Catfish

Servings: 4 / Cooking Time: 10 Mins.

Ingredients:

- 4 catfish fillets (6 oz. each)
- 1/2 tsp. salt
- 1/2 tsp. pepper
- 2 large eggs
- 1/3 C. Dijon mustard
- 2 tbsp. 2% milk
- 1/2 C. all-purpose flour
- 4 C. honey mustard miniature pretzels, coarsely crushed
- Cooking spray
- Lemon slices, optional

Directions:

1. Preheat air fryer to 325°. Sprinkle catfish with salt and pepper. Whisk eggs, mustard and milk in a shallow bowl. Place flour and pretzels in separate shallow bowls. Coat fillets with flour, then dip in egg mixture and coat with pretzels.

2. In batches, place fillets in a single layer on greased tray in air-fryer basket; spritz with cooking spray. Cook until fish flakes easily with a fork, 10-12 minutes. If desired, serve with lemon slices.

Keto Shrimp Scampi

Servings: 4 / Cooking Time: 10 Mins.

Ingredients:

- 4 tbsp. Butter
- 1 tbsp. Lemon Juice
- 1 tbsp. Minced Garlic
- 2 tsp. Red Pepper Flakes
- 1 tbsp. chopped chives, or 1 tsp. dried chives
- 1 tbsp. chopped fresh basil, or 1 tsp. dried basil
- 2 tbsp. Chicken Stock, (or white wine)
- 1 lb. (453.59 g) Raw Shrimp, (21-25 count)

Directions:

1. Turn your air fryer to 330F. Place a 6 x 3 metal pan in it and allow it to start heating while you gather your ingredients.

2. Place the butter, garlic, and red pepper flakes into the hot 6-inch pan.

3. Allow it to cook for 2 minutes, stirring once, until the butter has melted. Do not skip this step. This is what infuses garlic into the butter, which is what makes it all taste so good.

4. Open the air fryer, add butter, lemon juice,, minced garlic, red pepper flakes, chives, basil, chicken stock, and shrimp to the pan in the order listed, stirring gently.

5. Allow shrimp to cook for 5 minutes, stirring once. At this point, the butter should be well-melted and liquid, bathing the shrimp in spiced goodness.

6. Mix very well, remove the 6-inch pan using silicone mitts, and let it rest for 1 minute on the counter. You're doing this so that you let the shrimp cook in the residual heat, rather than letting it accidentally overcook and get rubbery.

7. Stir at the end of the minute. The shrimp should be well-cooked at this point.

8. Sprinkle additional fresh basil leaves and enjoy.

Poultry Recipes

Air Fryer Chicken Quesadilla

Ingredients:

- Soft Taco Shells
- Chicken Fajita Strips
- 1/2 C. sliced green peppers
- 1/2 C. sliced onions (I use the frozen fajita blend)
- Shredded Mexican Cheese
- Salsa (optional)
- Sour Cream (optional)
- Simple Living XL 5L Air Fryer

Directions:

1. Preheat Air Fryer on 370 degrees for about 3 minutes.
2. Spray pan lightly with vegetable oil.
3. Place 1 soft taco shell in pan.
4. Place shredded cheese on shell. (you can use as much or as little as you'd like.)
5. Lay out fajita chicken strips so they are in a single layer.
6. Put your onions and green peppers on top of your chicken.
7. Add more shredded cheese.
8. Place another soft taco shell on top and spray lightly with vegetable oil. (I put the rack that came with the air fryer on top of the shell to hold it in place. If you don't, the fan will suck it up. Trust me on this one!)
9. Set timer for 4 minutes.
10. Flip over carefully with large spatula.
11. Spray lightly with vegetable oil and place rack on top of shell to hold it in place.
12. Set timer for 4 minutes.
13. If it's not crispy enough for you, leave in for a couple of extra minutes.
14. Remove and cut into 4 slices or 6 slices.
15. Serve with Salsa and sour cream if desired.

Air Fryer Marinated Whole Chicken

Servings: 8 / Cooking Time: 55 Mins.

Ingredients:

- 1 3.5lb to 4lb whole chicken (giblets removed)
- 2 - 3 tbsp. oil
- 1 tsp. garlic powder
- ½ tbsp. Italian seasoning
- 1 tsp. chicken bouillon powder
- 1 tsp. parsley flakes
- 1 tsp. salt
- ½ tsp. white pepper
- 1 tsp. paprika

Directions:

1. Prepare Chicken

2. Check that giblets are removed then pat chicken dry with paper towel.

3. Method 1: Wet Marinade

4. Mix the spice blend with oil till combined.

5. Brush the marinade all over the chicken, don't forget to brush some in the cavity.

6. Cover chicken with cling film and let it marinate for up to 24 hrs in the refrigerator (if time permits)

7. Method 2: Dry rub

8. Brush oil all over chicken and inside the cavity. Gradually pour seasoning blend a little at a time till the chicken is completely covered in spice blend.

9. Gently pat it down with your fingers.

10. Cover with cling film wrap and let it marinate for up to 24 hrs in the refrigerator.

11. Time to Air fry

12. When the marinating time is up, Place marinated whole chicken in the air fryer basket breast side down.

13. Set temperature to 360°F / 180°C for 40 mins then flip over and cook for another 15 mins or until internal temperature reads 165°F / 74°C on an instant read meat thermometer. Let it rest for 5 mins before carving.

How To Make Chinese Egg Rolls

Ingredients:

- Filling
- 2 tbsp. peanut oil (or vegetable oil)
- 1 C. carrots , shredded
- 2 C. napa cabbage , thinly shredded
- 1 C. bean sprouts
- 3 tbsp. soy sauce
- 1 tsp. honey
- 4 cloves garlic , minced
- 1 tbsp. ginger , minced
- 1 lb. (450 grams) ground turkey (or chicken)
- 1 tbsp. hoisin sauce
- 1/4 tsp. black pepper
- 1/3 C. green onions , thinly sliced
- Egg rolls
- 25 egg roll wrappers 6 1/2 x 6 1/2 inches or 17 x 17 cm, thawed
- Vegetable oil for deep frying
- Dipping sauce (optional)
- Homemade sweet chili sauce (or store bought)
- Chinese dumpling sauce
- Homemade hoisin sauce (or store bought)

Directions:

1. Egg roll filling

2. Heat 1 tbsp. oil in a large nonstick skillet (or cast iron skillet) over medium-high heat until hot. Add the carrot and napa cabbage. Cook and stir for 2 minutes.

3. Add the bean sprouts and stir for 1 minute.

4. Add 1 tbsp. soy sauce and the honey. Cook and stir for another minute until the liquid has evaporated. Transfer everything to a plate to cool.

5. Add the remaining 1 tbsp. of oil and the garlic and ginger into the same skillet. Stir for 20 to 30 seconds, to release the fragrance.

6. Add the ground turkey (or chicken). Cook while chopping the ground meat into small bits with a spatula, until lightly browned.

7. Add the remaining 2 tbsp. of soy sauce and the hoisin sauce and black pepper. Stir and cook until the liquid is absorbed, 2 to 3 minutes. Transfer everything to a medium-sized bowl to cool.

8. Add the cooked vegetables and green onions to the bowl of ground turkey. Stir to mix well.

9. Wrap the egg rolls

10. To prepare the wrapping station: Add some water to a small bowl. Place the egg roll wrappers on a plate along with a spoon and the filling. Prepare a large plate or oven tray to hold the wrapped egg rolls and a cutting board for wrapping the egg rolls.

11. To wrap an egg roll, gently remove one egg roll sheet from the stack using both of your hands and place it on the cutting board, with a corner pointed toward you. Add 2 to 3 tbsp. of filling onto the lower end of the wrapper, making a 4-inch (10 cm) wide, tight and even mound. Tightly roll from the bottom corner toward the top, until about halfway up. Tightly fold the left and right corners of the wrapper

towards the center, so it looks like an opened envelope. Dip your finger into the water and brush the top corner of the wrapper. Tightly roll the egg rolls upward until it's completely sealed. Repeat the process, until you've used all the filling.

12. Although you can freeze the egg rolls at this stage, I personally prefer to cook them all and store the cooked ones so I only need to set up the deep frying equipment once. On the other hand, if you want to make the egg rolls in advance and serve them fresh at your party, you can freeze the egg rolls without cooking them. To do so, place the egg rolls on a baking sheet with gaps in between. Wrap them tightly with plastic wrap and store in the freezer until ready to cook. You can fry them directly from the freezer, with an additional 1 minute of fry time.

13. Cook the egg rolls

14. Prepare a baking sheet with a rack on top, for cooling the egg rolls.

15. Option 1 - To deep fry the egg rolls, heat 1-inch (2.5 cm) of oil in a deep medium pot or a dutch oven over medium heat to 350 F (177 C). If you do not have a thermometer, insert a wooden chopstick into the heated oil. You should see continuous tiny bubbles coming up around the chopstick. If the bubbles only come up here and there, the oil is not hot enough. If the bubbles are large and bursting to the surface, the oil is too hot.

16. Fry the egg rolls in batches of 5 to 6. Flip and move them occasionally for even browning. Fry until the egg rolls are golden, 5 to 6 minutes. Drain and transfer the egg rolls with a slotted spoon or wire spider onto the rack to let them cool. Repeat until you have cooked all the egg rolls.

17. Option 2 - To bake the egg rolls in the oven, preheat the oven to 400 degrees F (200 C). Place the egg rolls onto a lined baking sheet, seam-side-down, with about 2 fingers' width gap between. Generously spray oil on top. Bake for 9 minutes, or until the bottom turns a golden color. Flip the spring rolls and spray oil onto them again. Return the tray to the oven. Bake for another 6 to 8 minutes, until the other side is golden as well. Once done, let the egg rolls cool on a wire rack for 10 minutes before serving to maximize crispiness.

18. Option 3 - To fry the egg rolls in an air-fryer, preheat the air-fryer to 390 F (10 mins or so). Cook them in batches. Spread a few spring rolls in the basket without overlapping them. Spray with a thin layer of oil, or you can bake them without using any oil. Bake for 6 minutes, flip, and bake for another 5 minutes. Once done, let the egg rolls cool on a wire rack for 10 minutes before serving to maximize crispiness.

19. Serve the egg rolls hot with whichever dipping sauce(s) you prefer.

20. Store and reheat

21. You can store the cooked egg rolls and reheat them later. If stored and reheated properly, the egg rolls will be just as crispy as freshly fried.

22. To store the egg rolls, spread them on a wire rack and let them cool completely. The egg rolls will be

very hot inside once cooked, so it might take 1 to 2 hours for them to cool completely. Once cooled, you can store them in an airtight container or in a large ziplock bag. To get the best result, I prefer to spread the egg rolls in a single layer in a gallon ziplock bag and lay them flat in the fridge (or freezer). This way, the egg rolls won't overlap and get soggy.

23. You can reheat the egg rolls in the oven or in an air fryer. Bake them at 350 F (180 C) until hot, or for about 10 minutes or so. The rolls will remain crispy.

Gourmia Air Fryer Lemon Garlic Baked Drumsticks Recipe

Servings: 4 / Cooking Time: 50 Mins.

Ingredients:

- 3 cloves minced garlic
- ¼ c. soy sauce, low-sodium
- ¼ c. olive oil, extra-virgin
- 1 lemon juice
- Black pepper, freshly ground
- Kosher salt
- Pinch red pepper flakes, crushed
- 3 lbs. chicken drumsticks (about 8 pieces)

Directions:

1. In a large bowl, mix together the soy sauce, lemon juice, garlic, and oil.

2. Season the mixture with a pinch of red pepper flakes, salt, and pepper.

3. Add drumsticks into the bowl and toss to coat.

4. Put in refrigerator and allow about 30 minutes (or even up to overnight) to marinate.

5. Preheat the Gourmia air fryer at 450°. Transfer chicken to a large baking sheet and bake for 20-25 minutes, flipping halfway through until golden brown. When done, an internal temperature should read 165°.

6. Remove and serve hot.

Air Fryer Nashville Hot Chicken Hack

Ingredients:

- FOR THE CHICKEN:
- About 2-4 frozen pre-cooked breaded chicken breasts
- FOR THE NASHVILLE HOT SAUCE:
- 1/4 C. (60 g) butter
- 1/4 C. (60 ml) oil
- 1 tbsp. (15 ml) ground cayenne pepper , or 2 tbsp. for extra hot
- 2 tbsp. (30 ml) brown sugar
- 1 tsp. (5 ml) garlic powder
- 1 tsp. (5 ml) paprika
- 1 tbsp. (15 ml) Worcestershire sauce or soy sauce
- 1/2 tsp. (2.5 ml) salt , or to taste
- 1 tsp. (5 ml) black pepper
- FOR SERVING
- 6-8 slices (6-8 slices) white bread
- Pickles , whatever you prefer – bread & butter, dill, or both

Directions:

1. Make the Sauce: Combine all the sauce ingredients in a bowl or saucepan (butter, oil, cayenne pepper, brown sugar, garlic powder, paprika, Worcestershire or soy sauce, salt and pepper). Microwave or heat until butter is just melted (the hotter it is, the harder it will be to emulsify the spices in the liquids). Whisk thoroughly until smooth.

2. When the sauce is cooler, it doesn't separate as easily so we like to brush sauce on the chicken when the sauce is slightly cooler or room temperature. If you want your sauce warmer, then keep stirring or whisking the sauce as you brush the chicken so that you have as little separation of sauce/oil as possible. The warmer the sauce is, the more the spices will want to separate from the liquids.

3. Place the frozen breaded chicken breasts in the air fryer basket in a single layer. Make sure they aren't overlapping. No oil spray is needed.

4. Air Fry at 380°F/193°C for 10 minutes. Flip the chicken over.

5. Continue to Air Fry at 380°F/193°C for another 2 minutes. Check the chicken breasts and if needed, add another 2-3 minutes or until heated through and crispy to your preference.

6. Place chicken on top of white bread. Brush both sides of chicken with the hot sauce. Top with pickles and serve warm. Enjoy!

7. NOTES

8. Air Frying Tips and Notes:

9. No Oil Necessary. Cook Frozen – Do not thaw first.

10. Don't overcrowd the air fryer basket. Lay in a single layer.

11. Recipe timing is based on a non-preheated air fryer. If cooking in multiple batches of chicken back to

back, the following batches may cook a little quicker.

12. Recipes were tested in 3.7 to 6 qt. air fryers. If using a larger air fryer, the chicken might cook quicker so adjust cooking time.

13. Remember to set a timer to flip/toss as directed in recipe.

Air Fryer Orange Chicken From Frozen

Servings: 2 / Cooking Time: 15 Mins.

Ingredients:

♦ 10 oz. (240 g) Frozen Orange Chicken (about 2 C. worth)
♦ Sauce from the Packaged Frozen Orange Chicken

Directions:

1. Place the frozen orange chicken in the air fryer basket and spread out into a single even layer. No oil spray is needed. Set the sauce aside (do not sauce the chicken yet).

2. Air Fry at 400°F/205°C for 8 minutes. Shake and flip the chicken pieces over and then continue to cook at 400°F/205°C for another 2-4 minutes or until heated through and crispy.

3. Warm the orange sauce in microwave for 1 minute or on stovetop for 2-3 minutes on medium heat. Toss cooked chicken with sauce and serve.

4. NOTES

5. Air Frying Tips and Notes:

6. No Oil Necessary. Cook Frozen – Do not thaw first.

7. Shake or turn if needed. Don't overcrowd the air fryer basket.

8. Recipe timing is based on a non-preheated air fryer. If cooking in multiple batches of orange chicken back to back, the following batches may cook a little quicker.

9. Recipes were tested in 3.7 to 6 qt. air fryers. If using a larger air fryer, the orange chicken might cook quicker so adjust cooking time.

10. Remember to set a timer to shake/flip/toss as directed in recipe.

Air Fryer Chicken Fajitas Recipe

Ingredients:

- 1 lb. Boneless Chicken breasts or boneless skinless chicken thighs (cut into bite sized strips)
- 1 tbsp. oil (See note 2)
- 2½ tbsp. Fajitas seasoning
- 1 Medium red bell pepper (cut into ¼ inch strips)
- 1 Medium green bell pepper (cut into ¼ inch strips)
- 1 Medium yellow or orange bell pepper (cut into ¼ inch strips)
- 1 Medium Onion (Sliced into ¼ inch strips)

Directions:

1. Season the chicken
2. Pat chicken strips dry, transfer to a clean bowl. Add the slices bell peppers and onion to the chicken.
3. Add the oil and fajitas seasoning to that chicken, peppers and onions. Toss to coat. Make sure everything is coated evenly.
4. Air fry
5. Transfer seasoned chicken, peppers and onion mix into the air fryer basket.
6. Set temperature to 390°F / 200°C and cook for 15 mins. Remember to toss the chicken fajitas with a spatula half way through cooking time.
7. Let it rest for 2 mins in the air fryer before serving.
8. NOTES
9. No need to preheat the air fryer.
10. Use just enough oil to coat the chicken and veggies. 1 tbsp. works for me especially when using chicken thighs. If you find that it's not well coated, you can use add ½ a tbsp. more making it a total of 1 ½ Tablespoons.

Air Fryer Chicken Nuggets

Servings: 4 / Cooking Time: 8 Mins.

Ingredients:

- 3-4 boneless chicken breasts
- 2 eggs, beaten
- 100g breadcrumbs, (approx)
- Seasoning of your choice, eg; 1tsp smoked paprika, 1tsp garlic granules, 1/2 tsp salt, 1/2 tsp pepper.

Directions:

1. Cut chicken breasts up into small chicken nugget-sized chunks.
2. Set up a chicken nugget breading station of three bowls. Add the beaten egg to one bowl, mix the seasoning with the breadcrumbs, add to a different bowl, and put the raw chicken pieces in another bowl.
3. Using kitchen tongs, dip the chicken in the beaten egg, then roll it in the seasoned breadcrumbs. Place in air fryer basket.
4. Repeat with each piece of chicken. Depending on the size of your air fryer, you may need to cook in 2 separate batches.
5. Cook at 200°C (390°F) for 8 to 10 minutes. Check the chicken nuggets are cooked through before serving.
6. NOTE
7. Instead of eggs, you can dip the chicken in melted butter.

Air Fryer Stuffed Turkey Breast "roll" With Bacon, Spinach/kale, & Parmesan

Servings: 8 / Cooking Time: 45 Mins.

Ingredients:

- 2 1.5 lb. (680g) deboned raw turkey breasts
- salt , to taste
- black pepper , to taste
- FILLING:
- 4 slices bacon , cut into bite sized pieces
- 4 oz. (113 g) mushrooms , sliced
- 1/2 small onion , diced
- 2 cloves garlic , minced
- 2 C. (480 ml) chopped fresh kale or spinach (if frozen use 1 cup, thawed, then squeeze out water)
- 1/2 tsp. (2.5 ml) dried thyme , oregano or rosemary (or 1/2 tbsp. fresh)
- 1/4 tsp. (1.25 ml) dried sage or 1/2 tbsp. fresh chopped
- 1/4 tsp. (1.25 ml) kosher salt , or to taste
- 1/4 tsp. (1.25 ml) black pepper , or to taste
- 1/4 C. (25 g) shredded parmesan cheese or crumbled feta

Directions:

1. MAKE THE FILLING:

2. Heat pan on medium-high heat and add bacon. Cook until bacon starts to become crispy. Add onion, garlic and mushrooms. Cook until mushrooms shrink and release moisture.

3. Add kale or spinach and cook until softened. Add dried herbs, salt and pepper and stir. Remove pan from heat.

4. Add the cheese and give it a good stir. Set filling aside.

5. PREPARE THE TURKEY BREASTS:

6. Place a sheet of plastic wrap on top of each turkey breast and lb. thinner into an even thickness, about 1/2-inch thick.

7. Place the turkey breasts skin side down. Divide the filling between the two turkey breasts. Fold one edge of turkey breast over and roll. Tie turkey breast. Repeat with the second breast. Season top of tied breasts with additional salt and pepper.

8. Coat air fryer basket/tray with oil spray. Unless you have an oven style air fryer, cook the breasts one at a time in the air fryer. If you have a larger oven-style air fryer, you'll be able to cook both at the same time. Don't have them touching. Leave space between them. (If cooking one at a time, refrigerate the second stuffed breast until ready to cook.)

9. Air Fry at 360°F/180°C for 20 minutes. Flip the stuffed breast(s) over.

10. Continue to Air Fry at 360°F/180°C for another 10-20 minutes or until internal temperature of turkey reaches 165°F the thickest part. Allow to rest for 5 minutes and then slice and serve.

Slow Cooker Chicken Tacos

Ingredients:

- ♦ FOR THE CHICKEN
- ♦ 2 lb. chicken , preferrably boneless and skinless (*see head note)
- ♦ 1 C. tomato sauce or salsa
- ♦ 2 tbsp. Worcestershire sauce or soy sauce
- ♦ 1 tbsp. chili powder
- ♦ 1 tsp. ground cumin
- ♦ 1 tsp. onion powder
- ♦ 1 tsp. garlic powder
- ♦ 1/2 tsp. salt , or more to taste
- ♦ Fresh cracked black pepper , to taste
- ♦ 1/2 tsp. chipotle powder , or to taste (optional, for spicy flavor)
- ♦ FOR THE TACOS
- ♦ 12 soft or hard taco shells *see note below
- ♦ lettuce, shredded cabbage, tomato, cheese, salsa, sour cream, or other favorite toppings

Directions:

1. Add all the ingredients into the slow cooker (chicken, tomato sauce or salsa, Worcestershire sauce, chili powder, cumin, onion powder, garlic powder, salt & pepper, and optional chipotle powder). Stir to completely coat the chicken with the spices & sauce.

2. Slow cook 6-8 hours on low or 4-5 hours on high.

3. Take the chicken pieces out of the slow cooker, cut into 1-2 inch pieces, then place back in the slow cooker. Shed with a couple forks to break up the chicken.

4. Taste the chicken and add more salt if needed.

5. See note below about taco shell options. Build your tacos and serve or have everything in bowls for everyone to make their own tacos.

6. NOTES

7. For soft tortillas, we love to char them a little over a burner, or at least to warm them in the microwave. After warming, cover them in a kitchen towel, paper towels, or foil to help keep them softened and not dry out.

8. For hard shells, warming them in the oven or air fryer a bit before serving makes them extra tasty.

Air Fryer Blackened Chicken Tenders

Servings: 4 / Cooking Time: 12 Mins.

Ingredients:

- 1 lb. chicken cut into strips
- 1 tbsp olive oil
- 2 tsp chili powder
- 1 tsp cayenne pepper
- 1 tsp paprika
- 1/2 tsp salt
- 1/2 tsp ground pepper

Directions:

1. Place the chicken strips in a medium bowl and toss with olive oil, coating each piece of chicken.

2. Sprinkle chili powder, cayenne pepper, paprika, salt and pepper over the coated chicken. Toss the chicken in the bowl until the seasonings have evenly covered each piece of chicken.

3. Place the chicken in the air fryer basket, spread out so they aren't overlapping or stacked.

4. Cook at 380 degrees F for 12 minutes, flipping chicken tenders halfway through cooking.

Reheat Rotisserie Chicken In Air Fryer

Servings: 8 / Cooking Time: 8 Mins.

Ingredients:

- 1 3.5lb to 4lb Rotisserie chicken (whole or cut up into pieces)
- Serving suggestion
- Air fryer mushrooms air fryer vegetables

Directions:

1. Reheating it whole in basket

2. Place whole chicken in the basket. Set temperature to 360°F / 180°C. Air fry for 8 to 10 mins or until warmed through. Remember to flip half way through cooking time.

3. Reheating it whole on rotisserie spit

4. Pass the spit rod through the chicken and set temperature to 360°F / 180°C and cook for 5 to 6 mins or until heated through.

5. Reheating when carved into parts

6. Place chicken pieces in the basket and air fry at 360°F / 180°C for 6 to 8 mins or until heated through. Flip chicken half way through.

Air Fryer Chicken Parmesan

Servings: 4 / Cooking Time: 40 Mins.

Ingredients:

♦ 2 large boneless chicken breasts
♦ Salt
♦ Freshly ground black pepper
♦ 40 g plain flour
♦ 2 large eggs
♦ 100 g panko bread crumbs
♦ 25 g freshly grated parmesan
♦ 1 tsp. Dried oregano
♦ 1/2 tsp. Garlic powder
♦ 1/2 tsp. Chilli flakes
♦ 240 g marinara/tomato sauce
♦ 100 g grated mozzarella
♦ Freshly chopped parsley, for garnish

Directions:

1. Carefully butterfly chicken by cutting in half widthwise to create 4 thin pieces of chicken. Season on both sides with salt and pepper.

2. Prepare dredging station: place flour in a shallow bowl and season with a large pinch of salt and pepper. Place eggs in a second bowl and beat. In a third bowl, combine bread crumbs, parmesan, oregano, garlic powder, and chilli flakes.

3. Working with one piece of a chicken at a time, coat in flour, then dip in eggs, and finally press into panko mixture making sure both sides are coated well.

4. Working in batches as necessary, place chicken in basket of air fryer and cook at 200°c for 5 minutes on each side. Top chicken with sauce and mozzarella and cook at 200°c for 3 minutes more or until cheese is melty and golden.

5. Garnish with parsley to serve.

Pickle-brined Fried Chicken

Servings: 4 / Cooking Time: 47 Mins.

Ingredients:

- 4 chicken legs bone-in and skin-on, cut into drumsticks and thighs (about 3½ pounds)
- pickle juice from a 24-oz. jar of kosher dill pickles
- ½ C. flour
- salt and freshly ground black pepper
- 2 eggs
- 2 tbsp. vegetable or canola oil
- 1 C. fine breadcrumbs
- 1 tsp. salt
- 1 tsp. freshly ground black pepper
- ½ tsp. ground paprika
- 1/8 tsp. cayenne pepper
- vegetable or canola oil in a spray bottle

Directions:

1. Place the chicken in a shallow dish and pour the pickle juice over the top. Cover and transfer the chicken to the refrigerator to brine in the pickle juice for 3 to 8 hours.

2. When you are ready to cook, remove the chicken from the refrigerator to let it come to room temperature while you set up a dredging station. Place the flour in the a shallow dish and season well with salt and freshly ground black pepper. Whisk the eggs and vegetable oil together in a second shallow dish. In a third shallow dish, combine the breadcrumbs, salt, pepper, paprika and cayenne pepper.

3. Pre-heat the air fryer to 370°F.

4. Remove the chicken from pickle brine and gently dry it with a clean kitchen towel. Dredge each piece of chicken in the flour, then dip it into the egg mixture, and finally press it into the breadcrumb mixture to coat all sides of the chicken. Place the breaded chicken on a plate or baking sheet and spray each piece all over with vegetable oil.

5. Air-fry the chicken in two batches. Place two chicken thighs and two drumsticks into the air fryer basket. Air-fry for 10 minutes. Then, gently turn the chicken pieces over and air fry for another 10 minutes. Remove the chicken pieces and let them rest on plate – do not cover. Repeat with the second batch of chicken, air frying for 20 minutes, turning the chicken over halfway through.

6. Lower the temperature of the air fryer to 340°F. Place the first batch of chicken on top of the second batch already in the basket and air fry for an additional 7 minutes. Serve warm and enjoy.

Air Fryer Whole Roast Chicken

Servings: 4-6 / Cooking Time: 1 Hour

Ingredients:

- 1 whole chicken (up to 2kg, depending on the size of your air fryer)
- 1tbsp olive oil
- 1tsp smoked paprika
- 1tsp dried mixed herbs
- 1tsp garlic granules/salt

Directions:

1. Using a brush, coat the chicken in olive oil.

2. Mix the seasoning together and paste it all over the chicken. Make up some more spice mix if there isn't enough to coat the whole chicken.

3. Place the chicken in the air fryer basket, breast side down. Cook at 180°C for 45 minutes. Check on it once or twice to ensure it is cooking ok and not burning.

4. At 45 minutes, turn the chicken over so that it is breast side up. Cook for a further 15 minutes.

5. Check the chicken has cooked through. You can pierce it with a sharp knife to see if the juices run clear - or, my preferred way, use a meat thermometer to check the internal temperature. If it isn't cooked through, return it to the air fryer and cook for some more time, checking on it every so often.

6. NOTE

7. Serve with chips, potato wedges, rice, salad - anything goes with chicken.

8. Experiment with different seasoning rubs, and you can change up the taste each time.

Snacks & Side Dishes Recipes

Zucchini Pizza Bites In The Air Fryer

Servings: 4 / Cooking Time: 11 Mins.

Ingredients:

♦ 1/2-1 Zucchini
♦ Salt To taste
♦ Garlic powder To taste
♦ ½ - 1 C. Pizza sauce
♦ ½ - 1 C. Mozzarella cheese
♦ Favorite pizza toppings

Directions:

1. Cut the zucchini into ½ inch thick slices

2. Season each slice with a pinch of salt and let it sit for 5 minutes to remove moisture.

3. Add Garlic powder to taste and any of other of your favorite pizza inspired seasonings (Italian seasoning, basil, etc).

4. Place a piece of parchment paper in the air fryer basket. Layer the zucchini in the air fryer basket, spray with a little oil, and cook for 8 minutes at 320 °F, or until the zucchini is tender and roasted to your liking.

5. Spoon on pizza sauce, cheese, and favorite toppings onto each zucchini bite.

6. Cook for 3 minutes at 400 °F, or until the cheese is melted to your liking.

7. Remove and enjoy!

8. NOTES

9. Make sure to use parchment paper for easy clean up!

Air Fryer Kale Chips

Ingredients:

- ½ bunch Kale (about 8 Stalks)
- ½ tbsp. oil (You can also use oil spray)
- ⅛ tsp. salt
- ½ tsp. ranch powder (or favorite seasoning)

Directions:

1. Remove the middle stalk from each leaf, cut leaves into preferred sizes and wash

2. Drain leaves with a colander before transferring to a paper towel lined tray to absorb more water. Gently dab the top with some paper towel till the leaves have been well dried.

3. Drizzle or Spray on some oil, Toss to coat the leave, sprinkle on some salt and ranch seasoning, toss again to coat.

4. Spread on the air fryer rack, do not overcrowd, a little overlap is allowed. Put an air fryer rack over it to prevent leaves flying around while it bakes.

5. Bake at 380°F / 194°C for 4-5 mins. Shake the basket half way through.

6. NOTES

7. Let the leaves dry completely before tossing in oil.

8. Feel free to use other seasonings.

9. If you pull out the basket to shake half way through and you notice some leaves already crispy, you can take those out and continue baking the rest.

Air Fryer Garlic Mushrooms

Servings: 2 / Cooking Time: 15 Mins.

Ingredients:

- 8 oz. (227 g) mushrooms , washed and dried
- 1-2 tbsp. (15-30 ml) olive oil
- 1/2 tsp. (2.5 ml) garlic powder
- 1 tsp. (5 ml) Worcestershire or soy sauce
- Kosher salt , to taste
- Black pepper , to taste
- Lemon wedges (optional)
- 1 tbsp. (15 ml) chopped parsley
- Equipment
- Air fryer

Directions:

1. Cut mushrooms in half or quarters (depending on preferred size). Add to bowl then toss with oil, garlic powder, Worcestershire/soy sauce, salt and pepper

2. Air fry at 380°F for 10-12 minutes, tossing and shaking half way through.

3. Squeeze lemon and top with chopped parsley.

Air Fried Dorito Cheese Bites

Servings: 2 / Cooking Time: 6 Mins.

Ingredients:

- 3/4 C. flour divided
- 1 egg whisked
- 4-8 Babybel cheeses frozen
- 1-3 handfuls of Doritos depending on how strong you want the Dorito flavor to be

Directions:

1. Before you begin, make sure that you freeze Babybel cheese for at least 1-2 hours.

2. Prepare 3 separate shallow bowls. One, ½ C. of flour. Second, 1 whisked egg. Third, crushed Doritos with ¼ C. of flour, mixed together.

3. Prepare the air fryer basket by placing a sheet of air fryer parchment paper inside. (If you aren't using air fryer parchment paper, remember to spray the air fryer basket).

4. Unwrap the cheese bites. Cover each cheese bite in the flour, egg wash, then Doritos mixture. Cover it in the egg wash again, then in the Dorito mixture again.

5. Press down on the cheese so that the chip sticks to the cheese.

6. Place the cheese inside and lightly spray with oil.

7. Cook at 370°F/188°C for 3 minutes. Flip the cheese, and cook for an additional 3 minutes.

Air Fryer Tater Tots

Ingredients:

♦ 16 oz. potato tots

Directions:

1. Preheat the Air Fryer to 400 degrees Fahrenheit.

2. Prepare the lining of the basket with parchment paper or by spraying with olive oil.

3. Add the tater tots into the basket of the Air Fryer in a single layer.

4. Cook on 400 degrees Fahrenheit for 15 minutes, flipping every 5 minutes. Add additional one minute increments for extra crispy tots.

Air Fryer Jalapeño Poppers

Ingredients:

♦ 10 Medium jalapeno peppers (Washed)
♦ 8 oz. cream cheese (room temperature)
♦ ¼ C. bacon bits
♦ ¼ C. Shredded cheddar cheese

Directions:

1. Prepare the peppers

2. Cut the peppers in half lengthwise, use a spoon to remove the seeds and membrane. Leave that stem intact. Set peppers aside.

3. Prepare the filling

4. Mix the cream cheese and bacon bits together. Leave out the shredded cheddar cheese.

5. Assemble the poppers

6. Fill each pepper with the cream cheese mixture. Repeat process till all the peppers are stuffed with cream cheese.

7. Top each pepper with some shredded cheddar cheese. Transfer to air fryer basket or tray.

8. Air fry

9. Set temp to 380°F / 180°C and air fry for 5 to 6 mins or until the cheese topping in melted.

Air Fryer French Toast

Ingredients:

- 4 slices medium thickness bread
- 2 eggs
- 80ml milk
- 40ml double cream (optinal)
- 1 tsp cinnamon
- 1 tsp vanilla extract
- Optional toppings (berries, icing sugar, maple syrup)

Directions:

1. Slice the bread into halves, quarters or lengthwise into 'soldiers' and lay flat in a shallow dish (you may need to do this in batches).

2. Whisk the eggs with the milk, cream (if using), cinnamon and vanilla extract.

3. Pour the egg mixture over the bread and leave to soak for a few minutes, turning it over halfway.

4. While the bread is soaking, preheat the air fryer to 180°C/350°F

5. Carefully transfer the soaked bread to the air fryer basket and air fry for 8 to 10 minutes, turning halfway.

6. If at the end of the air frying time the bread is not crisp enough, turn the temperature up to 200°C/400°F and air fry for a further 1 minute on each side.

7. Serve as it is or with some fresh berries, bananas, maple syrup or a sprinkling of icing sugar.

Simply The Best Air Fryer Roast Potatoes

Ingredients:

- 8 medium potatoes (Maris Piper)
- 1 tbsp olive oil

Directions:

1. Preheat airfryer to 180C/350F.

2. Peel and chop up potatoes. The smaller you cut them up the quicker they will cook.

3. Spray/brush with 1tbsp of oil - make sure they are all coated.

4. Put potatoes in air fryer basket and slide into the air fryer.

5. Cook for 25 minutes. Check on them at regular intervals and give them a good shake about.

Air Fryer Bacon Wrapped Corn On The Cob

Servings: 4 / Cooking Time: 16 Mins.

Ingredients:

♦ 4 Fresh corn on the cob
♦ ½ lb. Bacon (about 8 strips)
♦ ¼ C. barbecue sauce (optional)

Directions:

1. Prepare the corn

2. Remove husks if needed. Part corn dry if wet from rinsing or condensation.

3. Method 1

4. Wrap whole corn with 1 or 2 bacon rashers. 2 would be ideal if you like bacon in every bite.

5. Method 2

6. Cut corn on the cob into half. Then wrap each strip of bacon around it, securing with a cocktail stick or just placing seam side down in the air fryer basket.

7. Air fry

8. Place bacon wrapped corn on the cob in the air fryer basket seam side down if not using cocktail sticks.

9. Set temperature to 400°F / 200°C and cook for 16 mins flipping half way through. By this time the corn is ready if and that bacon is crispy if you you want the bacon more crispy cook for another 2 to 3 mins.

10. You can brush with some bbq sauce in the last 2 mins of cooking if you like.

11. For frozen corn on the cob

12. Let the frozen corn thaw completely then pat dry before wrapping with bacon then cook in the air fryer for up to 18 mins flipping half way through. Add more time as needed.

13. NOTES

14. I don't recommend using thick cut bacon for bacon wrapped corn on the cob but if you do, you'll need to cook for longer.

15. Fresh corn is recommended for this recipe to get the joy of biting into juicy sweet corn.

16. You can wrap the bacon on a full ear of corn. However cutting each ear of corn makes it easier for me to manage.

17. The corn should be fully cooked at about 15 mins. If the bacon hasn't crisped up to your liking cook for another 2- 3 minutes.

18. You can use toothpicks to secure the bacon or place seam side down when cooking. If you do use toothpicks, remember to take them out before serving.

Air Fryer Brussels Sprouts Recipe

Ingredients:

♦ 2 C. Brussels sprouts sliced lengthwise into ¼" thick pieces (see notes)
♦ 1 tbsp. olive oil OR maple syrup See note.
♦ 1 tbsp. balsamic vinegar
♦ 1/4 tsp. sea salt

Directions:

1. In a bowl, toss together the Brussels, oil or maple syrup, vinegar, and salt.

2. Cook at 400F for 8-10 minutes, shaking (and checking their progress) after 5 minutes and then at 8 the minute mark. You're going for crispy and browned, but not burnt!

3. NOTES

4. I can't stress enough how important it is to get ¼" thick pieces. Thicker slices will not cook fully. Slice the sprouts lengthwise. Depending on the size of your Brussels sprouts, that might mean cutting them in half, thirds, or more.

5. If you prefer softer Brussels sprouts, soak the slices in water for 10 minutes. Then, drain them, pat them dry, season them, and proceed with the recipe.

6. Use maple syrup for an oil free option. Just note that if you ditch the oil, the finished product won't be quite as crispy as the version with oil. But it's still delicious!

7. Calorie count is for the recipe with oil, because it's my favorite way to make these!

8. Leftovers will keep in an airtight container in the refrigerator for 3-4 days. You can serve leftovers warm or cold.

9. To reheat, either pop them into the microwave or the air fryer. In the air fryer, reheat these at 350° F for 5-7 minutes.

Killer Garlic Fries With Rosemary

Servings: 8 / Cooking Time: 25 Mins.

Ingredients:

♦ 1 28 oz. bag Alexia House Cut Fries with Sea Salt
♦ 1/3 C. canola oil
♦ 1/4 C. pressed garlic
♦ 1 tbsp. minced fresh rosemary
♦ 1 tbsp. minced parsley
♦ 1 tsp. kosher salt
♦ 1/2 tsp. freshly ground black pepper

Directions:

1. Preheat the oven to 400°F.

2. Spread the fries evenly on a baking sheet and bake for 15-20 minutes or until crisp, stirring halfway during cooking.

3. While the fries are baking, mix the canola oil with the garlic and rosemary and 1/2 tsp. of the kosher salt. (This step can be done ahead of time.)

4. Remove the fries from the oven and transfer to a large bowl with the garlic, rosemary and oil mixture and season with the remaining kosher salt and ground pepper. Toss well with tongs until combined and serve immediately.

5. NOTES

6. To make in an air fryer: Cook the fries in the air fryer at 400°F for 15-20 minutes, then toss with the garlic and oil mixture as directed above.

Air Fryer Garlic And Herb Potatoes

Servings: 4 / Cooking Time: 20 Mins.

Ingredients:

- 1kg new potatoes
- 2-3 sprigs rosemary
- Handful fresh parsley
- 2 tbsp garlic granules/powder
- 2 tsp salt
- 2 tbsp of olive oil

Directions:

1. Chop the potatoes into even-sized chunks, halving the medium ones and quartering the large ones.

2. Finely chop the parsley and the rosemary (leaves only).

3. Place the potatoes in a large bowl, and sprinkle over the chopped herbs, the garlic granules and salt. Drizzle over with olive oil and mix until all potatoes are well-coated.

4. Cook in air fryer at 200°C for 20 minutes, shaking after 10 minutes. If you have a smaller air fryer, you may have to cook for longer or in 2 small batches.

5. NOTES

6. While fresh garlic can be used, garlic granules make it much easier to ensure every potato is evenly garlicky.

Christmas Flapjack

Servings: 4 / Cooking Time: 30 Mins.

Ingredients:

- 225 g porridge oats
- 170 g soft brown sugar
- 1/2 tsp bicarbonate of soda
- 85 g plain flour
- 170 g melted butter
- 425 g jar mincemeat

Directions:

1. Mix the oats, flour, sugar and bicarbonate together and then stir in the butter.

2. Press half this mixture into the base of a 30 cm x 17 cm x 2 cm tin. Spread the mincemeat over this and then carefully scatter the remaining mixture over the top.

3. Bake in a pre-heated oven 180 degrees C/gas 4 for 25-30 minutes or until golden brown. Allow to cool before slicing into bars. Store in an air-tight container.

Easy Crispy Air Fryer Grilled Cheese Sandwiches

Servings: 2 / Cooking Time: 5 Mins.

Ingredients:

- 4 pieces thick moist bread
- butter
- 2 slices cheese

Directions:

1. Butter the outside side of each slice of bread. Place two of the bread slices in the air fryer, buttered side down. Place cheese on each of the bread slices in the air fryer, then top with the second slice of bread, buttered side up.

2. Cook at 350°F/175°C for 6-8 minutes, flipping halfway thru cooking. If you want a little more toasting, turn the air fryer up to 400°F/200°C for an additional 1-2 minutes.

3. Serve warm. Perfect for dipping in soup!

4. NOTES

5. For best results, use a thicker, more moist bread, like Grandma Sycamore's brand. If your air fryer fan is too powerful and is blowing the bread off the top, try inserting a few toothpicks to keep it from blowing off.

Air Fryer Boiled Eggs

Servings: 4 / Cooking Time: 10 Mins.

Ingredients:

- 4 eggs (cook as many as you need)

Directions:

1. Add room temperature eggs to the basket of your air fryer, and leave some space between them so that there is room for the hot air to circulate. Use a metal rack if needed to fit more in.

2. Set the air fryer temperature at 150C. Cook according to how well done you want your eggs (starting at 8 minutes for runny, up to 12 minutes for hard boiled).

3. At the end of the cooking time remove from the air fryer basket and plunge into an ice bath or into a bowl of cold water – this will prevent the eggs from continuing to cook.

4. Once they have cooled down a little and can be handled, remove the shell.

Vegetables & Vegetarian Recipes

Air Fryer Potatoes

Ingredients:

♦ 3 yukon gold potatoes quartered
♦ 1 tsp. olive oil
♦ 1/8 tsp. paprika
♦ 1/8 tsp. garlic powder
♦ Salt and pepper to taste
♦ Cooking spray

Directions:

1. Preheat the air fryer 380°F.

2. Toss the potatoes in a bowl with the olive oil, paprika and garlic powder. Season with salt and pepper, and toss to coat.

3. Place the potato wedges in the basket of the air fryer, without over crowding the pan. Cook for 8 minutes, then use tongs to flip and cook for an additional 5-7 minutes.

4. Remove and enjoy immediately with ketchup, if desired

5. NOTES

6. Storage: Store any leftovers in an airtight container. They will last about 3-4 days in the fridge. To reheat, just place in the airfryer at 360°F for 1-2 minutes or in a toaster oven. You can also reheat in the microwave but the potatoes won't retain their crispy texture that way.

7. Substitutes: For best results, follow the recipe as is. However you can switch out the spices if you'd like and use other types of potatoes.

8. Equipment: I just bought the NuWave air fryer a couple months ago and I used this to make this recipe and many more recipes. It's easy to use with guides on the appliance, easy to clean up and I've been very happy with the results!

9. * Please note the nutrition label does not include any dip or sauce.

Air Fryer Parmentier Potatoes

Servings: 4 / Cooking Time: 18 Mins.

Ingredients:

- 2 lbs potatoes (Russet, Irish, Idaho Maris Piper would work)
- 2 tsp. Salt divided
- 1 tsp. dried Parsley
- 1 tsp. dried Oregano
- ½ tsp. Rosemary
- 1 tsp. garlic powder
- 2 tbsp. oil

Directions:

1. Prepare potatoes
2. Wash and scrub potatoes then cut into cubes.
3. Parboil
4. Transfer potatoes into pot, add water and 1 tsp. of salt and bring to boil for 5 to 7 mins
5. Drain the parboiled potatoes.
6. Air fryer instructions
7. Transfer drained potatoes into a bowl, add the oil, remaining salt and herbs then toss to coat the potatoes.
8. Transfer coated potatoes to air fryer basket and roast at 400°F / 200°C for 15 to 18 mins
9. When the cooking time is up, serve immediately.
10. Oven
11. Preheat oven to 425°F / 220°C / Gas mark 7
12. Lightly grease the baking sheet then transfer coated potatoes to the baking sheet.
13. Bake for 15 mins, turn potatoes to the other side and bake for another 15 mins or until cooked through. Serve with your favorite side dish.

Air-fryer Cumin Carrots

Servings: 4 / Cooking Time: 15 Mins.

Ingredients:

- 2 tsp. coriander seeds
- 2 tsp. cumin seeds
- 1 lb. carrots, peeled and cut into 41/2-inch sticks
- 1 tbsp. melted coconut oil or butter
- 2 garlic cloves, minced
- 1/4 tsp. salt
- 1/8 tsp. pepper
- Minced fresh cilantro, optional

Directions:

1. Preheat air fryer to 325°. In a dry small skillet, toast coriander and cumin seeds over medium heat 45-60 seconds or until aromatic, stirring frequently. Cool slightly. Grind in a spice grinder, or with a mortar and pestle, until finely crushed.

2. Place carrots in a large bowl. Add melted coconut oil, garlic, salt, pepper and crushed spices; toss to coat. Place on greased tray in air-fryer basket.

3. Cook until crisp-tender and lightly browned, 12-15 minutes, stirring occasionally. If desired, sprinkle with cilantro.

Air Fryer Green Beans

Servings: 4-6 / Cooking Time: 8-16 Mins.

Ingredients:

- 1 lb. fresh green beans
- 1 tbsp. olive oil
- 1/2 tsp. kosher salt
- 1/4 tsp. freshly ground black pepper

Directions:

1. Heat an air fryer to 375°F. Meanwhile, trim the stem end from 1 lb. green beans. Transfer to a large bowl. Add 1 tbsp. olive oil, 1/2 tsp. kosher salt, and 1/4 tsp. black pepper, and toss to combine.

2. Air fry in batches if needed: Add the green beans to the air fryer basket and arrange into a single layer. Air fry until the green beans are crisp-tender, 8 minutes. If you prefer your green beans a little more tender, give the basket a toss to redistribute the beans, then cook for 2 minutes more.

Air Fryer Tofu Bites

Ingredients:

♦ 14 oz. (397 g) firm or extra firm tofu , (1 block) drained
♦ 1 tsp. (5 ml) lemon pepper
♦ 1/2 tsp. (2.5 ml) garlic powder
♦ 1/2 tsp. (2.5 ml) salt
♦ oil spray , for coating
♦ Sauce for dipping: soy sauce , bbq sauce, teriyaki sauce, chili garlic sauce

Directions:

1. Preheat air fryer at 400°F for 5 minutes.

2. Gently squeeze or press-out excess water from the tofu block. Cut tofu into 1" cubes.

3. Add tofu cubes to bowl. Spray evenly with oil around all sides. Sprinkle half the amount of spices: lemon pepper, garlic powder, and salt evenly around all the tofu cubes. Gently stir or toss. Repeat with another layer of light oil spray and remainder of spices.

4. Air Fry at 400°F for 10 minutes. Gently flip over the tofu cubes or shake the basket so tofu can tumble and turn. Continue to Air Fry for another 10 minutes or until golden brown.

5. Check the texture of the tofu. If you want it more crispy, then Air Fry for additional 5-10 minutes OR until the tofu is to your liking. We like our tofu extra crispy with an outside crust so we'll cook it for an extra 7 minutes.

6. Allow to slightly cool and dip in your favorite sauce.

Air Fryer Bacon Wrapped Potatoes With Baby Potatoes

Servings: 8 / Cooking Time: 15 Mins.

Ingredients:

- 32 baby potatoes
- 1 lb. Thin sliced bacon (about 16 slices)
- ½ tsp. black pepper (optional)
- Spicy sour cream dip
- ¼ C. sour cream
- 2 tbsp. Mayonnaise
- 2 tsp. sriracha sauce (use less to reduce the heat)
- 2 tsp. apple cider vinegar
- salt & black pepper to taste

Directions:

1. Make the sauce
2. Mix all the sauce ingredients together till well combined then set aside on that counter if using immediately. Put in the refrigerator if you aren't making the potatoes immediately
3. Prepare the bacon
4. Cut bacon in half crosswise and set aside
5. Prepare potatoes
6. Wash potatoes thoroughly and dry with paper towel no need to peel.
7. Assemble it all
8. Wrap each baby potatoes with half a slice of bacon and secure seam with tooth picks or cocktail sticks.
9. Repeat process till all potatoes have been wrapped.
10. Sprinkle with black pepper if using
11. Air fry
12. Place 16 bacon wrapped potatoes in the air fryer basket or the amount that fits.
13. Set temperature to 400°F / 204°C and bake for 13 - 15 mins flipping half way through. Let the potatoes rest for a minute in the air fryer then remove and cook second batch.
14. Serve with your favorite dipping sauce.
15. NOTES
16. Recipe serves 8 and can easily be halved.
17. Use cold bacon. It's easier to cut cold bacon without stretching and distorting the shape.
18. No need to preheat the air fryer. However start checking the second batch at 12 mins
19. Do not overcrowd your basket. Cook in batches if needed. I use a 5.8qt air fryer 16 fits in mine at a time. Put whatever amount that will fit in yours without overcrowding the basket.

Air Fryer Eggplant

Servings: 2-4 / Cooking Time: 15 Mins.

Ingredients:

- 1 oz. Parmesan cheese (about 1/2 firmly packed C. grated on a Microplane or 1/3 C. store-bought)
- 1 C. panko breadcrumbs
- 1/2 tsp. Italian seasoning
- 1/2 tsp. garlic powder
- 1 large egg
- 1 tbsp. water
- 1 medium eggplant (about 1 pound)
- 3/4 tsp. kosher salt
- Cooking spray
- Marinara sauce, for dipping

Directions:

1. Heat an air fryer to 400°F. Meanwhile, finely grate 1 oz. Parmesan cheese and place in a shallow bowl. Add 1 C. panko breadcrumbs, 1/2 tsp. Italian seasoning, and 1/2 tsp. garlic powder and mix to combine. Whisk 1 large egg and 1 tbsp. water toegether in a second shallow bowl.

2. Trim the stem from 1 medium eggplant. Cut the eggplant crosswise into 1-inch-thick rounds, then cut the rounds into 1-inch-wide fries. Sprinkle with 3/4 tsp. kosher salt and toss to combine.

3. Working with one at a time, dip each piece of eggplant into the beaten egg and turn to coat. Dredge in the panko mixture, pressing to adhere, and place on a plate.

4. Lightly coat the air fryer basket with cooking spray. Working in batches if needed, place a single layer of fries in the basket (they can be touching but should not be stacked). Air fry for 8 minutes. Flip the fries and air fryer until lightly browned all over, about 7 minutes more. Serve immediately with marinara sauce for dipping.

Lemony Green Beans

Servings: 4 / Cooking Time: X Mins.

Ingredients:

- 1 lb. green beans, washed and destemmed
- 1 lemon
- Pinch of salt
- Black pepper to taste
- 1/4 tsp. oil

Directions:

1. Put green beans in air fryer.

2. Add a few squeezes of lemon.

3. Add salt and pepper.

4. Drizzle oil over top.

5. Cook in Avalon Bay Air Fryer at 400 degrees for 10-12 minutes.

Air Fryer Brussels Sprouts Apple Pecan Salad

Servings: 5 / Cooking Time: 15 Mins.

Ingredients:

- 1 lb. Brussels sprouts trimmed and halved
- 2 tablespooons olive oil
- 1/4 tsp. kosher salt
- 1/4 tsp. freshly ground pepper
- 1/2 tsp. cayenne pepper
- 1 C. sliced apple I used honeycrisp
- 1/2 C. dried cranberries
- 1/4 C. chopped pecans
- 1/3 C. red wine vinaigrette homemade or store-bought

Directions:

1. Preheat the air fryer to 350°F/175°C for 5 minutes.

2. In a bowl, mix together to evenly coat the brussels sprouts with olive oil, salt, pepper, and cayenne pepper.

3. Place the prepared brussels sprouts in the air fryer basket and cook for 10-15 minutes. Halfway through cooking, open drawer and stir contents and mix in the sliced apple, dried cranberries, and chopped pecans. Continue roasting until sprouts and apples reach desired crispiness.

4. Remove from the air fryer basket and transfer to a serving platter. Drizzle with red wine vinaigrette. Serve immediately.

The Best Easy Air Fryer French Fries Recipe

Servings: 6 / Cooking Time: 20 Mins.

Ingredients:

- 3 large russet potatoes
- 2-3 tbsp. olive oil
- Sea salt and pepper, to taste

Directions:

1. Using a mandoline, slice the potatoes into fries. I don't worry too much about the size of fry I am making- some are bigger, and some are smaller. That's fine!

2. Next, place your spuds in a nice cool water bath. Completely submerge the fries in water.

3. Let fries sit one hour. This helps to remove excess starch and will help the fries crisp up more in the oven.

4. Preheat air fryer to 375 degrees.

5. After an hour, drain the water, and pat fries dry with a paper towel.

6. Toss with a couple tbsp. of olive oil, salt and pepper.

7. Add fries to bottom of air fryer basket, making sure they are all on the same level (don't stack them on top of each other.)

8. Cook 13 minutes, until crispy and golden brown.

9. Place on a baking sheet lined with paper towels and a cooling rack over it.

10. Place in warm oven (set to the minimum temperature, not over 250 degrees) and let rest while other batches of fries are cooking.

11. Serve hot and enjoy.

Air Fryer Crispy Breaded Broccoli Bites

Servings: 2 / Cooking Time: 12 Mins.

Ingredients:

- 1/2 lb. (227 g) fresh broccoli , cut into bite sized pieces (about 2 cups)
- 1/2 tsp. (2.5 ml) salt , or to taste
- fresh cracked black pepper
- 1/2 tsp. (2.5 ml) garlic powder
- 1 egg , beaten
- 1/2 C. (54 g) bread crumbs (Italian style or Japanese panko)
- 2 tbsp. (30 ml) grated parmesan cheese
- Optional Dips: hot sauce, ranch, bbq sauce, etc.

Directions:

1. Pre-heat air fryer at 360°F for 5 minutes.

2. Add broccoli to a bowl. Season with salt, pepper and garlic powder evenly over broccoli. Add beaten egg to the broccoli and stir to coat the broccoli.

3. In another bowl combine the bread crumbs and parmesan cheese Dip broccoli in the bread crumb mix and shake off excess. Spray all sides of the breaded broccoli with oil spray. Dry breading might fly around in air fryer and burn, so make sure to coat any dry spots.

4. Spray air fryer basket or tray with oil and place broccoli in a single layer in the basket/tray.

5. Air Fry at 360°F for 5-8 minutes. Gently flip and spray any dry spots with oil spray.

6. Air Fry at 360°F for additional 3-5 minutes or until they are crispy golden brown OR to your preferred texture. Serve warm with your favorite dip.

Air Fryer Wontons Appetizer

Ingredients:

- 1 package won ton wrappers
- 1 package coleslaw mix
- 2 tbsp. soy sauce
- 2 tbsp. butter

Directions:

1. How to Make the Mixture
2. In a large cast iron pan, melt the butter.
3. Add coleslaw mix and cook for about 5 minutes.
4. Add the soy sauce and continue cooking for another minute.
5. Season with salt and pepper if necessary.
6. Remove from heat and allow mixture to cool before assembling the wontons.
7. How to Assemble the Wontons
8. Lay the wonton wrappers on top of a piece of parchment paper.
9. Place about a tbsp. of the cooled coleslaw mixture in one corner of the wonton wrapper.
10. Dip your finger in a small bowl filled with water and spread a very little amount of the water over the edges of the wonton.
11. Fold one corner of the wonton wrapper catty-corner to the opposite corner creating a triangle shape pressing the sides together firmly squeezing out any air bubbles.
12. Place on a baking tray that's been covered with parchment paper and cover with a damp paper towel while you continue forming the rest of the wontons, adding them to the tray and keeping covered also with the dampened paper towel.
13. How to Air Fry the Wontons
14. Preheat the air fryer by setting the temperature to 375 degrees for 10 minutes.
15. Once the air fryer is preheated, spray the basket with non-stick cooking spray and add a few wontons to the basket and let cook for 3 to 4 minutes or until the wontons are golden brown.
16. Repeat the process until all the wontons are cooked.
17. Once cooked remove from the basket and let cool before enjoying.

Air Fryer Potato Chips

Servings: 4 / Cooking Time: 30 Mins.

Ingredients:

♦ 4 large Russet Potatoes
♦ 1 tbsp olive oil
♦ 1 tsp salt

Directions:

1. Wash the potatoes and pat dry.

2. Use a mandolin slicer or sharp knife and slice the potatoes into ⅛ inch slices.

3. Place the potato slices in a medium bowl of water. Let them soak for at least 30 minutes. The water will get cloudy as they soak.

4. After they have soaked, drain potatoes and rinse them again in cold water and pat dry with a paper towel.

5. Toss the potato slices in the olive oil, and season with salt. Working in batches, place the slices in a single layer in the air fryer basket.

6. Set your oven to Air Frying at 380 degrees F. Cook for 10-15 minutes, depending on the thickness of the cut. Shake the basket halfway through cook time. Cook the chips until they begin to turn golden brown.

7. Remove the chips and place them on a sheet of paper towels until they cool. Garnish with fresh parsley flakes or season with salt to taste.

Potato Rolls

Servings: X / Cooking Time: 40 Mins.

Ingredients:

- 1 medium baking potato (about 175g)
- 125ml hot water (42C)
- 2 large eggs, at room temperature
- 125g sugar
- 2 1/4 tsp rapid rise yeast (10g package)
- 110g unsalted butter, at room temperature, plus more for brushing
- 1 tsp fine salt
- 380g plain flour
- Equipment: 2 (23cm) round or square cake tins

Directions:

1. Cook the potato in a microwave on HIGH until soft so it squeezes easily, using the designated baked potato setting or for up to 15 minutes. Scoop out the inside pass the warm potato through a potato ricer or food mill into a large bowl (you should have about 200g mashed potato).

2. Stir the hot water, eggs, half the sugar and the yeast into the potato. Add 280g of the flour and the salt and mix with a wooden spoon to make a sticky, shaggy dough. Cover the bowl tightly with cling film and set aside in a warm place until the dough doubles in volume, about 1 1/2 hours.

3. Beat the 110g of butter with the remaining sugar in a standing mixer fitted with the paddle attachment until light and fluffy. Switch to the dough hook and add the risen dough to the creamed butter. Continue to mix on low until the butter and dough come together, about 1 minute (stop the mixer and scrape down the bowl if needed; the dough will be very sticky). Gradually add the remaining flour, about 35g at a time, to make a shaggy dough that pulls away from the side of the bowl. Continue kneading on medium speed until the dough is smooth but still tacky, about 3 to 4 minutes.

4. Turn the dough onto a lightly floured work surface and knead by hand until it is smooth and no longer tacky, one to two minutes more. (If the dough is still sticky, gradually add 40g flour.)

5. Brush a large bowl with butter and turn the dough around in the bowl to coat lightly. Cover the bowl tightly with cling film, trace a circle the size of the dough ball on the plastic, and note the time. Leave to rise at room temperature until doubled in size, about one and a half hours.

6. Generously butter two 23-cm round or square cake tins. Turn the dough out of the bowl and pat into a rectangle about 35cm by 20cm, gently pressing out excess air. Divide the dough into 32 equal portions, using a pizza wheel. (Divide the dough in half lengthwise, then in half crossways. Cut each of those four sections into 8 equal-sized rolls.)

7. Tuck the edges of each piece of dough under to make round rolls and place seam-side down in the prepared tins, leaving a little space in between each roll (see Cook's Note). Cover the tin with buttered cling film and set aside in a warm place until the rolls rise almost to the rim of the tin and have more than doubled in size, about 45 minutes.

8. Position a rack in the centre of the oven and preheat the oven to 190°C / gas mark 5.

9. Bake the rolls until golden brown and puffy, and an instant read thermometer inserted into the centre of a roll registers 85°C, about 40 minutes. Remove the rolls from the oven and quickly brush the tops with soft butter.

10. Cool the rolls in the tin for about ten minutes before turning them out onto a rack in one piece. Cool slightly. Serve warm or at room temperature in one piece or pulled apart as individual rolls.

Air Fryer Zucchini Fries

Servings: 4 / Cooking Time: 20 Mins.

Ingredients:
- 3 medium zucchini
- 1 tsp salt adjust to taste
- 1 tsp ground black pepper adjust to taste
- 1 tbsp Italian seasoning
- 1/2 C. flour
- 2 large eggs
- 1 C. bread crumbs panco or italian bread crumbs
- 1/3 C. parmesan cheese
- 2 tbsp spray oil

Directions:
1. On a large plate, combine flour, salt, pepper, and Italian seasoning.

2. In a separate, small bowl, whisk eggs together. Set aside.

3. In a medium-sized bowl, combine bread crumbs and parmesan cheese.

4. Cut zucchini into 3-inch long fries. Dip each fry into flour seasoning, followed by egg and parmesan bread crumbs.

5. Coat the air fryer basket with cooking oil and place zucchini fries into the basket in a single layer. Spray the zucchini with light coat of cooking oil. Air fry at 400°F for 9 minutes.

Favorite Air Fryer Recipes

Air Fryer Halloween Mummy Dogs

Ingredients:

- 8 oz. (227 g) refrigerated crescent dough or crescent dough sheets , see headnote
- 8 hot dogs
- mustard
- ketchup or hot sauce
- oil spray

Directions:

1. Unroll the crescent dough. Cut into 3/8"-1/2" (9mm-13mm) wide strips.

2. Pat the hot dogs dry (helps keep the dough from slipping around while rolling).

3. Wrap a couple pieces of dough around each hot dog to look like bandages. Criss-cross them occasionally and make sure to leave a separation of the bandages on one end for the face. Stretch the dough if needed. Word of Caution: Don't wrap too many layers on top of each other or else the underlying ones may not cook all the way. Repeat for the remaining dough and hot dogs.

4. Lightly spray the ends of the wrapped hot dogs with oil spray. Spray the air fryer basket with oil spray. Lay the wrapped hot dogs face-side up in the air fryer basket or tray, making sure the mummies aren't touching (cook in batches if needed).

5. Air Fry at 330°F (166°C) for 6 minutes. Gently wiggle to loosen from the baskets.

6. Air Fry at 330°F (166°C) for another 1-3 minutes or until crescent dough is golden, and cooked through.

7. Dot the face with mustard and ketchup (or hot sauce) for the eyes and any other desired facial features. Enjoy!

Air Fryer Tater Tot Breakfast Bake With Kielbasa Sausage

Servings: 2 / Cooking Time: 20 Mins.

Ingredients:

- 24 frozen tater tots , (potato puffs) approximately (about 1/2 pound-227g)
- 4-5 inches (10-13 cm) kielbasa or pre-cooked sausage link , sliced 1/2-inch thick and cut into half moons (about 1/4 lb.(113g) worth)
- 3 large eggs
- 2 tbsp. (30 ml) milk
- 1/4 C. (30 g) cheese
- 2 green onions , chopped
- salt , to taste
- pepper , to taste
- oil spray

Directions:

1. Coat the base of 6-8" accessory baking pan with oil spray. Spread tater tots in an even layer and spray with oil.

2. Air Fry the tots at 380°F/195°C for 5-7 minutes, or until the tots are golden.

3. Add the sausage pieces to the tater tot, nestling it in-between the tots. Air Fry at 380°F/195°C for another 2-3 minutes.

4. In bowl beat together the eggs, milk, cheese, green onions, salt, and pepper. Pour egg mixture into pan with the tater tots and sausage. Gently spread egg mixture to coat in-between tater tots & sausage.

5. Lower temperature and Air Fry at 320°F/160°C for about 8-10 minutes. If needed, leave the bake in the air fryer to continue cooking in the residual heat while the air fryer is turned off. Allow to cool slightly and enjoy!

Breakfast Frittata

Servings: X / Cooking Time: X Mins.

Ingredients:

- Philips Airfryer
- Philips Airfryer baking accessory
- 3 eggs
- ½ Italian sausage
- 4 cherry tomatoes (in half)
- 1 tbsp. olive oil
- Chopped parsley
- Grano Padano cheese (or parmesan)
- Salt/Pepper

Directions:

1. Preheat the AirFryer to 360 degrees

2. Place the cherry tomatoes and sausage in the baking accessory and bake at 360 degrees for 5 minutes.

3. In a small bowl, whisk the remaining ingredients together.

4. Remove the baking accessory from the AirFryer and add the egg mixture, making sure it is even. Bake for another 5 minutes.

Air Fryer Mini Calzones

Servings: 16 / Cooking Time: 12-15 Mins.

Ingredients:

- All-purpose flour, for rolling out the dough
- 1 lb. pizza dough, at room temperature at least 1 hour
- 1 C. pizza sauce, plus more for dipping
- 8 oz. shredded part-skim mozzarella cheese
- 6 oz. thinly sliced pepperoni or mini pepperoni, chopped

Directions:

1. On a lightly floured surface, roll out the pizza dough until 1/4-inch thick. Use a 3-inch round cutter or a large glass to cut out 8 to 10 rounds of dough. Transfer the rounds to a parchment paper-lined baking sheet. Gather up the dough scraps, then reroll and repeat cutting out rounds until you have 16.

2. Top each round with 2 tsp. of sauce, 1 tbsp. of cheese, and 1 tsp. of pepperoni. Working with one dough round at a time, fold in half, then pinch the edges together to seal. When each calzone is sealed, use a fork to crimp the edges closed to further seal.

3. Heat the airfryer to 375°F. Working in batches of 4, air fry the calzones until golden brown and crisp, about 8 minutes. Serve with additional pizza sauce for dipping, if desired.

Air Fryer Sausage Stuffing

Servings: 4 / Cooking Time: 15 Mins.

Ingredients:

- 6 oz. (170 g) box stuffing mix (not 12 oz.)
- 4 tbsp. (60 g) butter
- 1/2 onion , diced
- 2 stalks celery , diced
- 1/2 lb. (227 g) raw sausage
- 1/2 tsp. (2.5 ml) garlic powder , or to taste
- 1 1/2 C. (360 ml) chicken or beef broth or water
- 1-2 tbsp. (15-30 ml) chopped fresh or dried herbs (parsley, sage, rosemary, etc) , optional
- Black pepper , to taste
- Salt , to taste if needed
- 2 tbsp. (30 g) additional melted butter , for brushing
- Optional Additional Stuffing Extras:
- chopped bacon, chopped nuts, dried fruit, mushrooms, etc.

Directions:

1. Heat medium skillet on medium high-heat. Melt butter and add onions and celery. Cook until onions are soft.

2. Add sausage and break it up into small pieces (a meat chopper makes quick work of this). Stirring occasionally, cook until browned. Add garlic powder, optional herbs, black pepper, salt, and broth (and add any other optional stuffing extras) and then stir. Heat to a low boil.

3. Remove from heat. Add stuffing and mix lightly.

4. Spray oil or brush butter inside of 7" accessory bucket or baking dish.

5. Fill prepared 7" accessory bucket or baking dish with stuffing and spread into an even layer. Cover with foil.

6. For Oven Style Air Fryers: Place the stuffing dish on lowest rack of the air fryer. For Bucket Style Air Fryers: place the stuffing dish in the air fryer.

7. Air Fry at 350°F/175°C for 10 minutes, covered with foil. Then remove foil and brush with melted butter. Leave the stuffing uncovered in the air fryer.

8. Continue to Air Fry for another 2-5 minutes or until the top is crisp to your liking. Remove from air fryer and serve warm.

Air Fryer Pizza Rolls

Servings: 4 / Cooking Time: 6 Mins.

Ingredients:

- Homemade Pizza Rolls
- 1 pizza dough Pillsbury Thin Crust
- 1/2 C. mozzarella cheese shredded
- 1/2 C. pizza sauce pizza sauce or marinara sauce
- 1 egg
- 1/4 C. pepperonis cut into small pieces
- 1 tbsp water
- Frozen Totino's Pizza Rolls
- 20 pizza rolls Totino's brand is my favorite

Directions:

1. Homemade Pizza Rolls

2. Roll out the pizza dough and use a large cookie cutter to create 5" circles.

3. Add a tbsp. of pizza sauce to the middle of the dough.

4. Sprinkle mozzarella cheese, pepperonis, and additional toppings on the pizza sauce. Careful to not overfill the rolls.

5. Whisk the egg and water together. Use a brush to brush the inner edges of the dough. Fold over the dough and then press down to seal the edges. Use a fork to seal the edges completely. Continue with the remainder of the pizza rolls.

6. Place the pizza rolls into the prepared Air Fryer basket. Prepare the basket with nonstick spray or with parchment paper. Line the basket with the pizza rolls in a single layer. Air fry the pizza rolls on 350 degrees Fahrenheit for 6-8 minutes, flipping halfway through.

7. Serve with extra pizza sauce or marinara sauce for dipping.

8. Frozen Totino's Pizza Rolls

9. Preheat the air fryer to 380 degrees Fahrenheit.

10. Add the pizza rolls to the bottom of the basket and set the cook time for 6 minutes. Flip the pizza rolls halfway at the 3 minute mark.

11. Set the pizza rolls to the side for 2 minutes before serving, they're HOT.

Air Fryer Cinnamon Rolls

Ingredients:

- 1 oz. cream cheese
- 1 tbsp. unsalted butter
- All-purpose flour
- 1 (8-ounce) tube refrigerated crescent roll dough
- 1/4 C. packed light brown sugar
- 1 1/2 tsp. ground cinnamon
- 1/4 C. powdered sugar
- 1 tbsp. whole or 2% milk

Directions:

1. Cut 1 oz. cream cheese into 8 pieces. Place in a medium bowl and let sit at room temperature to soften while you prepare the cinnamon rolls.

2. Place 1 tbsp. unsalted butter in a small microwave-safe bowl and microwave until melted, about 30 seconds. (Alternatively, melt the butter on the stovetop in a small saucepan.) Let cool slightly. Meanwhile, heat an air fryer to 325°F.

3. Add 1/4 C. packed light brown sugar and 1 1/2 tsp. ground cinnamon to the butter and stir to combine.

4. Cut a sheet of parchment paper about the size of the air fryer basket or tray and place on a work surface. Unroll 1 tube crescent roll dough onto the parchment. Gently press the seams together with your fingers. (It doesn't have to be perfect.) Spread the cinnamon-sugar mixture evenly onto the dough, leaving a 1/2-inch border. Gently press into the dough. Starting at a long side, tightly roll up the dough. Use your fingers to tightly press and seal the seam. Arrange seam-side down and cut crosswise into 8 pieces.

5. Arrange the rolls cut-side up, touching on another, on the parchment paper. Slide, still on the parchment, into the air fryer basket or onto the tray. Air fry until puffed and golden brown, 20 minutes. Let cool on the tray or in the basket for 5 minutes. Meanwhile, make the icing.

6. Add 1/4 C. powdered sugar to the cream cheese. Stir until smooth. Whisk in 1 tbsp. milk until thinned and smooth. Spread over the warm rolls and serve immediately.

Air Fryer Pizza Recipe

Ingredients:

- 1 lb. pizza dough, thawed if frozen
- Cooking spray
- 1 C. prepared pizza sauce
- 2 2/3 C. shredded Italian cheese blend
- Topping options:
- Pepperoni
- Sliced mushrooms
- Sliced peppers

Directions:

1. Divide 1 lb. pizza dough into 8 (2-ounce) pieces. If refrigerated, let sit on the counter until room temperature, at least 30 minutes.

2. Heat an air fryer to 375°F.

3. Press each piece of pizza dough into a round up to 6 1/2-inches wide, or 1/2 inch smaller than the size of your air fryer basket.

4. Coat the air fryer basket with cooking spray and carefully transfer one round of dough into the basket. (The basket will be warm.) Gently press the dough to the edges of the basket without touching the sides. Spread 2 tbsp. pizza sauce onto the dough, then sprinkle with 1/3 C. of the shredded cheese and top with any desired toppings.

5. Air fry until the crust is golden-brown and the cheese is melted, 10 to 12 minutes.

6. Carefully lift the pizza out of the air fryer basket with tongs or a spatula. Place on a cutting board and cut into wedges. Serve immediately and repeat with the remaining dough and toppings.

Air Fryer Pigs In A Blanket

Servings: 6 / Cooking Time: 8 Mins.

Ingredients:

- 24 cocktail hot dogs
- 1 can refrigerated crescent dough

Directions:

1. Pat the mini hot dogs dry with paper towel set aside.

2. Open the can of crescent dough, unroll crescent dough. You will have 8 scored triangles, cut each triangle into 3.

3. Place each cocktail hotdogs at the wider end of the triangle dough and roll towards the tip. Place tip side down on a tray.

4. Repeat process till all the hot dogs are wrapped.

5. Transfer from tray to air fryer basket and refrigerate the rest while the first batch cooks.

6. Bake at 330°F / 165°C for 8 to 10 mins or until golden brown. Remember to flip half way through cooking time. When the first batch is don't go ahead and cook subsequent batches.

7. Serve with your favorite dipping sauce.

8. NOTES

9. No need to preheat the air fryer. However subsequent batches will likely cook faster because the air fryer got preheated while cooking the first batch.

10. Do not overcrowd the basket.

11. Recipe can be doubled or tripled as needed.

Air Fryer Frozen Pizza Rolls

Servings: 3 / Cooking Time: 10 Mins.

Ingredients:

♦ 18 (170 g) Frozen Pizza Rolls

Directions:

1. Place the pizza rolls in the air fryer basket and spread out in to a single even layer. Don't overcrowd the basket or else they won't cook evenly. No oil spray is needed.

2. For Regular Sized Pizza Rolls: Air Fry at 380°F/193°C for 6-10 minutes or until golden and nearly starting to ooze their filling. Shake and flip over about halfway through cooking.

3. For Mini Sized Pizza Rolls: Air Fry at 380°F/193°C for 5-8 minutes or until golden and nearly starting to ooze their filling. Shake and flip over about halfway through cooking.

4. Let them rest for a couple minutes to cool off so the filling isn't dangerously hot. Be careful with that first bite!

5. NOTES

6. Air Frying Tips and Notes:

7. No Oil Necessary. Cook Frozen – Do not thaw first.

8. Shake or turn if needed. Don't overcrowd the air fryer basket.

9. Recipe timing is based on a non-preheated air fryer. If cooking in multiple batches of pizza rolls back to back, the following batches may cook a little quicker.

10. Recipes were tested in 3.7 to 6 qt. air fryers. If using a larger air fryer, the pizza rolls might cook quicker so adjust cooking time.

11. Remember to set a timer to shake/flip/toss as directed in recipe.

Air-fryer Ham And Egg Pockets

Servings: 2 / Cooking Time: 25 Mins.

Ingredients:

- 1 large egg
- 2 tsp. 2% milk
- 2 tsp. butter
- 1 oz. thinly sliced deli ham, chopped
- 2 tbsp. shredded cheddar cheese
- 1 tube (4 ounces) refrigerated crescent rolls

Directions:

1. Preheat air fryer to 300°. In a small bowl, combine egg and milk. In a small skillet, heat butter until hot. Add egg mixture; cook and stir over medium heat until eggs are completely set. Remove from the heat. Fold in ham and cheese.

2. Separate crescent dough into 2 rectangles. Seal perforations; spoon half the filling down the center of each rectangle. Fold dough over filling; pinch to seal. Place in a single layer on greased tray in air-fryer basket. Cook until golden brown, 8-10 minutes.

Air Fryer Kielbasa

Servings: 4 / Cooking Time: 8 Mins.

Ingredients:

- 1 Rope Smoked Kielbasa sausage (or cut into even slices)
- Serving suggestions
- ¼ C. Ketchup or Barbecue sauce (substitute with your favorite dipping sauce)
- Scrambled eggs
- Potatoes and peppers.

Directions:

1. cooking the whole rope of sausage

2. Place sausage rope in air fryer basket and set temperature to 380F / 190C and cook for 4 mins then flip over with a pair of kitchen tongs and cook for another 5 minutes.

3. for sliced Kielbasa

4. Place sausage slices in the air fryer and air fry at 380F / 190C for 4 mins then shake the basket and continue cooking for 3 to 4 mins or until you reach your desired level or browned.

Minnesota Mary With A Snit

Servings: 1 / Cooking Time: 15 Mins.

Ingredients:

- Ice
- 150ml infused pepper vodka, recipe follows
- 350ml tomato juice
- 1 tsp Worcestershire sauce
- 1 tsp celery salt
- 1 tbsp lemon juice
- 1 tsp hot sauce
- Pickled vegetables, onions, French beans, carrots, olives, celery, jalapeno, for garnish
- For the infused pepper vodka
- 235ml vodka
- 1 jalapeno red chilli
- 1 jalapeno green chilli
- 1 habenero chilli
- 1 poblano chilli
- 1 Serrano chilli

Directions:

1. For the cocktail:
2. Fill a large jug or bowl with ice, add the infused pepper vodka, tomato juice, Worcestershire sauce, celery salt, lemon juice and hot sauce. Mix well.
3. Garnish with pickled vegetables, onions, French beans, carrots, olives, celery and a jalapeno.
4. For the infused pepper vodka:
5. Cut all the peppers in half, add to the vodka, and let steep for 24 hours to 7 days depending on the heat desired.
6. Sieve through a coffee filter, and store in an air tight container.

Perfect Personal Pizzas In An Air Fryer

Servings: 1 / Cooking Time: 5 Mins.

Ingredients:

- 1 Stonegate Mini Naan Round
- 2 tbsp jarred pizza sauce
- 2 tbsp shredded pizza cheese or shredded Mozzarella
- 6 or 7 mini Pepperoni

Directions:

1. Top the mini naan round with the pizza sauce, shredded pizza cheese and mini pepperoni.
2. Place the topped personal pizza into the basket of an air fryer.
3. Set the air fryer to about 375 degrees F. "Fry" the pizza for between 5 to 7 minutes- or until cheese is completely melted and starting to brown. Serve immediately.

Breakfast Egg Rolls Air Fryer

Servings: 3 / Cooking Time: 10 Mins.

Ingredients:

- 2 eggs
- 2 T milk
- salt
- pepper
- 1/2 C shredded cheddar cheese
- 2 sausage patties or any other additional stir ins
- 6 egg roll wrappers
- 1 T olive oil
- water

Directions:

1. Cook sausage or substitute in a small skillet according to package. Remove from pan and chop into bite sized pieces.

2. Whisk together eggs, milk, a pinch of both salt and pepper. Add a tsp. of oil or a small pat of butter to pan, over medium/low heat. Pour in egg mixture and cook a few minutes, stirring occasionally to create scrambled eggs. Stir in sausage. Set aside.

3. Place egg roll wrapper on a work surface with points creating a diamond shape. Place about 1 T of cheese on bottom third of wrapper. Top with egg mixture.

4. Wet a finger or pastry brush with water and brush all edges of egg roll wrapper, this will help it seal.

5. Fold bottom point of egg roll wrapper up and over the filling, trying to get it as tight as you can. Next, fold in the sides, creating an envelope looking shape. Last, wrap the top point around the entire wrapper. Place seam side down and continue to assemble the remaining rolls.

6. Preheat air fryer to 400 F for 5 minutes.

7. Brush rolls with oil or spray them if you have a misto. Place in preheated basket. Set to 400 F for 8 minutes.

8. After 5 minutes, flip egg rolls over. Return egg rolls to air fryer for another 3 minutes.

9. Serve and enjoy!

Sweets & Desserts Recipes

Quick Air Fryer Maple Bars

Servings: 8 / Cooking Time: 10 Mins.

Ingredients:

- 1 Pillsbury buttermilk biscuits 8-count package
- MAPLE GLAZE
- 1/4 C. butter
- 1/2 C. brown sugar
- 3 tbsp milk
- 1 tbsp. corn syrup
- 2 tsp. maple extract
- 2 C. powdered sugar

Directions:

1. Preheat the air fryer at 400 °F for 5 minutes.
2. Stretch out the dough into an oblong/donut bar shape. You can stretch it out a lot further than you think, especially if you want more crunchy donuts. But if you want more biscuit donuts, only stretch it out a little.
3. Place the biscuits (about 4) in the air fryer basket- no need to spray the basket.
4. Cook for 5 minutes at 350 °F. You do not need to flip the donuts.
5. Let the donuts rest in the air fryer basket for about a minute or two. Then, transfer the donuts to a cooling rack or plate and let cool for 3-5 minutes.
6. Dip the donuts in the maple glaze. Let the glaze cool onto donuts for a couple of minutes or so. Then, enjoy!
7. MAPLE GLAZE
8. In a small saucepan, add the butter and brown sugar until mostly melted and combined.
9. Whisk in the milk and heat for about 5 minutes on medium heat, stirring often, until butter is melted and sugar is dissolved.
10. Remove the saucepan from the heat and add in corn syrup and maple extract.
11. Add the powdered sugar a 1/2 C. at a time to the saucepan. Whisk with each addition, until it is smooth. The glaze will get thicker and harden a. Keep adding powdered sugar until it reaches desired consistency.
12. Once all powdered sugar is added, keep maple glaze warm on the stove, whisking occasionally. Because it will begin to harden if you leave it sitting (but we do want it to get thick). Add 1-2 tsp more milk if needed to help thin it out if it gets too thick and hard.
13. Whisk the maple glaze a little before you dip the donuts in it.
14. NOTES
15. If you don't have corn syrup, you can replace it with honey. See recipe post for more substitution ideas.

Air Fryer Mug Cake

Ingredients:

- Kitchen Gadgets:
- Air Fryer
- Mug Cake Ingredients:
- 100 g Squares of Chocolate
- 100 g Squares of Chocolate broken
- 1 Tsp Butter heaped
- 1 Tsp Honey
- 1 Tsp Greek Yoghurt
- 1 Tbsp Self Raising Flour
- 1 Tsp Vanilla Essence optional
- 1 Tsp Cocoa Powder optional

Directions:

1. Into two ramekins add squares of chocolate along with your butter and honey.

2. Place in the air fryer and cook for 2 minutes at 120c/250f to melt the chocolate.

3. Stir and add in Greek yoghurt. It will now be lovely and creamy. Then add in your second lot of chocolate which will be crushed. Stir well.

4. Add in self raising flour and cocoa powder or vanilla if you are using it. Stir well.

5. Cook for 10 minutes at 180c/360f and enjoy!

Air Fryer French Toast Sticks Recipe

Servings: 2 / Cooking Time: 12 Mins.

Ingredients:

♦ 4 pieces bread whatever kind and thickness desired
♦ 2 Tbsp butter or margarine, softened
♦ 2 eggs gently beaten
♦ 1 pinch salt
♦ 1 pinch cinnamon
♦ 1 pinch nutmeg
♦ 1 pinch ground cloves
♦ 1 tsp icing sugar and/or maple syrup for garnish and serving

Directions:

1. Preheat Airfryer to 180* Celsius.

2. In a bowl, gently beat together two eggs, a sprinkle of salt, a few heavy shakes of cinnamon, and small pinches of both nutmeg and ground cloves.

3. Butter both sides of bread slices and cut into strips.

4. Dredge each strip in the egg mixture and arrange in Airfryer (you will have to cook in two batches).

5. After 2 minutes of cooking, pause the Airfryer, take out the pan, making sure you place the pan on a heat safe surface, and spray the bread with cooking spray.

6. Once you have generously coated the strips, flip and spray the second side as well.

7. Return pan to fryer and cook for 4 more minutes, checking after a couple minutes to ensure they are cooking evenly and not burning.

8. When egg is cooked and bread is golden brown, remove from Airfryer and serve immediately.

9. To garnish and serve, sprinkle with icing sugar, top with whip cream, drizzle with maple syrup, or serve with a small bowl of syrup for dipping.

Air Fryer Apple Pie Chimichangas

Ingredients:

- 3 Granny Smith apples, peeled and diced
- 1 C. water
- 1/4 C. corn starch
- 1 C. granulated sugar, divided
- 1 tsp ground cinnamon, divided
- 1/8 tsp ground nutmeg
- 1/2 tsp vanilla extract
- 1/8 tsp kosher salt
- 2 tsps fresh lemon juice
- 6 (10") flour tortillas, warmed
- 1/4 C. brown sugar
- 6 tbsps caramel sauce, divided, more for garnish if desired
- cooking spray
- vanilla ice cream (optional)

Directions:

1. Preheat air fryer to 400 degrees F.

2. Whisk together water and cornstarch in a small pan until no lumps remain. Over medium heat add 3/4 C. granulated sugar, 3/4 tsp. cinnamon, nutmeg vanilla, lemon juice and salt to the cornstarch mixture. Cook for two minutes, stirring occasionally; mixture will begin to thicken. Add apples and turn down the heat to low for 7-12 minutes or until the apples are soft. Remove from heat.

3. Place one tbsp. of caramel sauce on each warm tortilla and top with 1/2 C. of the apple mixture.

4. Tuck the ends and roll the tortilla to create a chimichanga. Secure with a toothpick if needed.

5. Spray air fryer basket with cooking spray and place two rolled chimichangas, seam side down, in the basket. Air fry for seven minutes.

6. Combine brown sugar and remaining granulated sugar in a shallow bowl.

7. Remove cooked chimichangas from basket and roll in cinnamon-sugar mixture. Top with vanilla ice cream and a drizzle of caramel sauce if desired.

Air Fryer Apple Turnovers

Ingredients:

- 2 Bramley apples or 3 smaller varieties (Granny Smiths, Royal Galas)
- 2 tbsp + 1 tbsp brown sugar
- 1 tsp ground cinnamon
- 1 tbsp lemon juice
- 320g puff pastry
- 2 tbsp milk

Directions:

1. Peel the apples and dice them into equal sizes.

2. Mix with 2 tbsp brown sugar, 1 tsp ground cinnamon and 1 tbsp of lemon juice.

3. Place in air fryer basket and cook at 190°C/380°F for 10 minutes, shaking at the halfway mark. If you prefer a smoother filing, you can stew the apples in a saucepan on the hob instead.

4. Cut the puff pastry into four equal sizes and lay out on a floured surface.

5. Divide the cooked apple between each pastry piece and place it on one side, leaving about 1cm of space around the edge.

6. With a pastry brush, baste the edges of each puff pastry with some milk before folding it over.

7. Press the edges down with a fork until all sides are stuck firmly together.

8. Baste the top of the apple turnover with some milk and pierce a hole in the top to allow the steam to escape.

9. Transfer each apple turnover to the air fryer basket. If your air fryer basket is prone to sticking, spray a little oil on it or use some baking paper.

10. Air fry at the same temperature for 10 to 12 minutes, carefully flipping over halfway. The puff pastry should be golden brown and flaky when it's ready.

Lotte Duncan's Christmas Brownies

Servings: 16 / Cooking Time: 35 Mins.

Ingredients:

- 400g caster sugar
- 4 large eggs
- 125g melted butter
- 100g plain flour
- 1 tsp baking powder
- 6 tbsp. cocoa powder
- 4 heaped tbsp. of Lotte's Boozy Mincemeat

Directions:

1. Line your tray with non-stick baking paper.

2. Preheat the oven to 170c (160c fan oven) Mk 5.

3. Whisk the sugar and eggs together either in a stand mixer or with an electric whisk and bowl. Whisk until pale and thick – this can take a few minutes. You really want to beat lots of air into them.

4. Now add the melted butter and whisk again.

5. Gently mix in the flour, baking powder and cocoa powder.

6. Finally stir in the boozy mincemeat.

7. Pour the mixture into your lined tray and bake in the oven for 30-35 minutes.

Apple Fries With Caramel Cream Dip

Servings: 8 / Cooking Time: 7 Mins.

Ingredients:

- 3 Pink Lady or Honeycrisp apples peeled, cored and cut into 8 wedges
- ½ C. flour
- 3 eggs beaten
- 1 C. graham cracker crumbs
- ¼ C. sugar
- 8 oz. whipped cream cheese
- ½ C. caramel sauce plus more for garnish

Directions:

1. Toss the apple slices and flour together in a large bowl. Set up a dredging station by putting the beaten eggs in one shallow dish, and combining the crushed graham crackers and sugar in a second shallow dish. Dip each apple slice into the egg, and then into the graham cracker crumbs. Coat the slices on all sides and place the coated slices on a cookie sheet.

2. Pre-heat the air fryer to 380°F. Spray or brush the bottom of the air fryer basket with oil.

3. Air-fry the apples in batches. Place one layer of apple slices in the air fryer basket and spray lightly with oil. Air-fry for 5 minutes. Turn the apples over and air fry for an additional 2 minutes.

4. While apples are cooking make caramel cream dip. Combine the whipped cream cheese and caramel sauce, mixing well. Transfer the Caramel Cream Dip into a serving bowl and drizzle additional caramel sauce over the top.

5. Serve the apple fries hot with the caramel cream dip on the side. Enjoy!

Hash Brown Recipe

Servings: 8 / Cooking Time: 15 Mins.

Ingredients:

♦ Large potatoes – 4 – peeled and finely grated
♦ Corn flour – 2 tablespoon
♦ Salt – to taste
♦ Pepper powder – to taste
♦ Chili flakes – 2 teaspoon
♦ Garlic powder – 1 tsp. (optional)
♦ Onion Powder – 1 tsp. (optional)
♦ Vegetable Oil – 1 + 1 teaspoon

Directions:

1. Soak the shredded potatoes in cold water. Drain the water. Repeat the step to drain excess starch from potatoes.

2. In a non-stick pan heat 1 tsp. of vegetable oil and saute shredded potatoes till cooked slightly for 3-4 mins.

3. Cool it down and transfer the potatoes to a plate.

4. Add corn flour, salt, pepper, garlic and onion powder and chili flakes and mix together roughly.

5. Spread over the plate and pat it firmly with your fingers.

6. Regrigerate it for 20 minutes

7. Preheat air fryer at 180C

8. Take out the now refrigerated potato and divide into equal pieces with a knife

9. Brush the wire basket of the air fryer with little oil

10. Place the hash brown pieces in the basket and fry for 15 minutes at 180C

11. Take out the basket and flip the hash browns at 6 minutes so that they are air fried uniformly

12. Serve it hot with ketchup

Avocado Fries

Ingredients:

- 2 large avocados
- ½ C. unsweetened almond milk , may also sub with 1 large egg if not vegan
- ½ C. superfine blanched almond flour
- For the coating:
- 1 C. unsweetened toasted shredded coconut , OR sub with crushed Simple Mills Grain-Free Sea Salt Almond Flour Crackers (or other favorite grain-free crackers like Hu's Kitchen Grain-Free Crackers)
- 1.5 tbsp Cajun seasoning spice mix OR smoked paprika
- Salt and pepper
- For the optional dip:
- ☐ C. vegan mayo
- 1 tbsp lemon juice
- ½ tbsp Cajun seasoning
- Salt and pepper to taste

Directions:

1. Use a large knife to cut your avocados in half and remove the pit from the middle. Cut the avocado into wedges or "fries".
2. Oven Method
3. Preheat oven to 400F. Line a large baking sheet with parchment paper.
4. Gather three wide shallow bowls. Place the almond milk in one bowl, the almond flour in the next bowl and combine the coating ingredients in the the third bowl.
5. Take one avocado slice, place it in the flour. Make sure it is fully coated in flour then gently shake to get rid of any excess flour.
6. Place it in the almond milk and again make sure it is fully coated and wet. You will find it easier if you use one hand for the first two steps and then the other hand for the breading, so you don't get too messy!
7. Finally place it in the coconut breading, making sure it is fully coated, then place on the baking pan.
8. Repeat until all the slices are coated. Place the baking sheet in the oven for 15-20 minutes until turning golden brown.
9. FOR THE DIP:
10. Make the dip by mixing all the ingredients together. Enjoy with the avocado fries!
11. Air Fryer Method
12. Place the breaded avocado sticks in a single layer in the air fryer basket, you will have to work in batches.
13. Lightly coat with cooking spray and cook for 8-12 minutes at 375F, or until golden and crispy, flipping halfway through.

Air Fry Frozen Sweet Plantains

Servings: 3 / Cooking Time: 7 Mins.

Ingredients:

- 11 oz. Goya Frozen plantains
- ¼ C. guacamole

Directions:

1. Air fryer
2. Remove plastic wrap. Place frozen plantains in a single layer in air fryer basket or rack.
3. Set Temperature to 350°F / 180°C and cook for 6 to 7 mins. You can flip half way through if making more that 1 pack at a time (11 oz. is one pack)
4. Serve with your favorite side dish or sauce. (See blog post for list of suggestions)
5. Oven method
6. Preheat oven to 350°F / 180°C / Gas mark 4. Remove plastic wrap and bake in baking sheet for 7 to 10 mins.
7. Serve and enjoy
8. Microwave
9. Remove plastic wrap, transfer to a microwave safe plate and microwave on high at 1 min intervals for 3 to 3 ½ mins or until warmed through. Let it stand for a minute before serving.

Tempura Fried String Beans

Ingredients:

- 1 C. all-purpose flour
- 1 C. cornstarch
- 1 tbsp. baking powder
- 1 tbsp. sugar
- Pinch salt
- 1 C. soda water
- 1 lb. string beans, washed, dried and trimmed
- 1/2 C. cranberry sauce

Directions:

1. Preheat oil in deep-fryer to 190C/Gas 5.

2. In a large bowl, add the flour, cornflour, baking powder, sugar and salt, and mix to combine. Whisk in the soda water and mix until a batter is formed.

3. Dip the beans in the batter being sure to shake off the excess. Fry the beans in batches for 2 to 3 minutes until crispy and golden. Remove to a paper towel-lined sheet tray to drain.

4. Arrange the beans on a platter and serve with warm cranberry sauce.

Air Fryer Avocado Fries

Ingredients:

- 2 avocados, slightly under ripe, this makes them easier to slice
- 1/3 C. almond flour
- 1 1/2 C. pork rinds, crushed
- 2 eggs, beaten
- 2 tbsp heavy cream
- 1/2 tsp paprika
- 1/2 tsp garlic powder
- 1/2 tsp salt & pepper
- 1/4 tsp each cumin and cayenne, optional

Directions:

1. Note, you will need 3 bowls or dishes for dredging
2. Peel avocado skin and slice long ways, evenly
3. Whisk cream and eggs together in one bowl
4. Combine almond flour and seasoning in one bowl
5. Add crushed pork rinds to one bowl
6. Dip avocado slice into the almond flour mixture coating evenly, then into the egg, then the pork rinds.
7. Place coated avocado slice into air fryer in a single layer.
8. Set air fryer at 400° for 5 minutes.
9. Flip avocado fries.
10. Set timer for 4-5 minutes. Remove.
11. Serve with your favorite dipping sauce or eat plain.

Canned Refrigerated Biscuits In Air Fryer

Servings: 8 / Cooking Time: 10 Mins.

Ingredients:

♦ 1 can refrigerated biscuits
♦ oil spray

Directions:

1. Spray the air fryer basket or racks with oil to keep the biscuits from sticking. We don't suggest using parchment paper underneath because you want maximum air flow under the biscuits to help them cook all the way though. The parchment paper prevents maximum air flow under the biscuits.

2. Lay biscuits in single layer of air fryer basket or racks. Make sure to space them out so they aren't touching & have room to rise & expand.

3. For Grand Or Large Biscuits (Homemade Buttermilk Style And Flaky Layers Style):

4. Air Fry at 330°F/165°C for about 6-7 minutes. Gently wiggle the biscuits to loosen from the baskets.

5. Continue to Air Fry for another 1-3 minutes, or until they are crispy brown and cooked through.

6. You can also flip the biscuits to finish off during the last 1-3 minutes of air frying (they won't be as pretty, but is neccesary in some air fryers).

7. For Smaller Size Biscuits (Homemade Buttermilk Style And Flaky Layers Style):

8. Air Fry at 330°F/165°C for 5 minutes. Flip the biscuits and air fry for another 2-4 minutes, or until they are crispy brown and cooked through.

Air-fryer French Toast C. With Raspberries

Servings: 2 / Cooking Time: 20 Mins.

Ingredients:

- 2 slices Italian bread, cut into 1/2-inch cubes
- 1/2 C. fresh or frozen raspberries
- 2 oz. cream cheese, cut into 1/2-inch cubes
- 2 large eggs
- 1/2 C. 2% milk
- 1 tbsp. maple syrup
- RASPBERRY SYRUP:
- 2 tsp. cornstarch
- 1/3 C. water
- 2 C. fresh or frozen raspberries, divided
- 1 tbsp. lemon juice
- 1 tbsp. maple syrup
- 1/2 tsp. grated lemon zest
- Ground cinnamon, optional

Directions:

1. Divide half the bread cubes between 2 greased 8-oz. custard cups. Sprinkle with raspberries and cream cheese. Top with remaining bread. In a small bowl, whisk eggs, milk and syrup; pour over bread. Cover and refrigerate for at least 1 hour.

2. Preheat air fryer to 325°. Place custard C. on tray in air-fryer basket. Cook until golden brown and puffed, 12-15 minutes.

3. Meanwhile, in a small saucepan, combine cornstarch and water until smooth. Add 1-1/2 C. raspberries, lemon juice, syrup and lemon zest. Bring to a boil; reduce heat. Cook and stir until thickened, about 2 minutes. Strain and discard seeds; cool slightly.

4. Gently stir remaining 1/2 C. berries into syrup. If desired, sprinkle French toast C. with cinnamon; serve with syrup.

Air Fryer Sweet Potato Chips

Servings: 2 / Cooking Time: 22 Mins.

Ingredients:

♦ 1 medium sweet potato
♦ 1 tbsp. canola oil
♦ 1 tsp. kosher salt
♦ 3/4 tsp. dried thyme leaves
♦ 1/2 tsp. freshly ground black pepper
♦ 1/4 tsp. paprika
♦ Pinch cayenne pepper (optional)
♦ Cooking spray

Directions:

1. Wash 1 sweet potato and dry well. Thinly slice 1/8-inch-thick with a knife or preferably on a mandoline. Place in a bowl, cover with cool water, and soak at room temperature for 20 minutes to remove the excess starch.

2. Drain the slices and pat very dry with towels. Place in a large bowl, add 1 tbsp. canola oil, 1 tsp. kosher salt, 3/4 tsp. dried thyme leaves, 1/2 tsp. black pepper, 1/4 tsp. paprika, and a pinch cayenne pepper if using, and toss to combine.

3. Lightly coat Instant Vortex Plus 7-in-1 Air Fryer Oven rotisserie basket with cooking spray. Air fry in batches: place a single layer of sweet potato slices in the rotisserie basket. Place the rotisserie basket in the air fryer and press rotate. Preheat the air fryer to 360°f and set for 22 minutes. Air fry until the sweet potatoes are golden brown and the edges are crisp, 19 to 22 minutes.

4. Transfer the chips to a paper towel-lined plate to cool completely, they will crisp as they cool. Repeat with air frying the remaining sweet potato slices.

Printed in Great Britain
by Amazon

20401522R00061